Islam has been more misunderstood than any other religion. In this book, long regarded as a classic, Frithjof Schuon explains the basis of Islamic belief 'from within'. He takes as his point of departure the theme that Islam is 'the meeting between God and Man' and expounds the Islamic view of life, the role of the Prophet and the Quran, and the nature of Sufism and the path of spiritual ascent. The author, described by T. S. Eliot as the most impressive writer in the field of comparative religion that he had encountered, studied Arabic and Arabic calligraphy and then explored for himself Islam and Buddhism in North Africa, India and Turkey.

UNDERSTANDING ISLAM

Other Mandala Books

THE ART OF MEDITATION by Joel Goldsmith
BUDDHISM: ITS DOCTRINE AND ITS METHODS by A. David-Neel
THE BUDDHIST WAY OF ACTION by Christmas Humphreys
COMPASSION YOGA by John Blofeld
CONCENTRATION by Mouni Sadhu
CREATIVE MEDITATION AND MULTI-DIMENSIONAL CONSCIOUSNESS by
    Lama Anagarika Govinda
ESSENTIALS OF INDIAN PHILOSOPHY by M. Hiriyanna
HARA by Karlfried Dürckheim
I CHING: THE CHINESE BOOK OF CHANGE, a translation by John Blofeld
INFINITE WAY by Joel Goldsmith
THE LIFE OF THE BUDDHA by H. Saddhatissa
MAN AND NATURE by S. H. Nasr
MANTRAS by John Blofeld
RAMANA MAHARSHI by T. M. P. Mahadevan
RŪMĪ: POET AND MYSTIC by R. A. Nicholson
SAMADHI by Mouni Sadhu
TAO TÊ CHING translated by Ch'u Ta-Kao
TAOISM: THE QUEST FOR IMMORTALITY by John Blofeld
THE WAY AND ITS POWER translated by Arthur Waley
A WESTERN APPROACH TO ZEN by Christmas Humphreys
ZEN BUDDHISM by Christmas Humphreys

Understanding Islam

FRITHJOF SCHUON

Translated by D. M. Matheson

Mandala Books
UNWIN PAPERBACKS
London
Boston   Sydney

First published in Great Britain by George Allen & Unwin 1963
Reprinted 1965
First published in Unwin Paperbacks 1976
Reprinted 1979

UNWIN ® PAPERBACKS
40 Museum Street, London WC1A 1LU

This translation © George Allen & Unwin (Publishers) Ltd
1963, 1976

British Library Cataloguing in Publication Data

Schuon, Frithjof
  Understanding Islam.
  1. Islam
  I. Title
  297   BP50   78-40579

  ISBN 0-04-297035-0

Printed in Great Britain by
Hazell Watson & Viney Ltd, Aylesbury, Bucks

Foreword

As may be inferred from its title the purpose of this book is not so much to give a description of Islam as to explain, one might say, why Moslems believe in it: in what follows, therefore, the reader is presumed already to have certain elementary notions about the religion of Islam such as can be found without difficulty in other books.

What we really have in mind in this as in previous works is the *scientia sacra* or *philosophia perennis*, that universal gnosis which always has existed and always will exist. Few topics are so unrewarding as conventional laments about the 'researches of the human mind' never being satisfied; in fact everything has been said already, though it is far from being the case that everyone has always understood it. There can therefore be no question of presenting 'new truths'; what is needed in our time, and indeed in every age remote from the origins of Revelation, is to provide some people with keys fashioned afresh—keys no better than the old ones but merely more elaborated—in order to help them to rediscover the truths written in an eternal script in the very substance of man's spirit.

This book is no more restricted to an exclusive programme than were our earlier writings. A number of digressions will be found which, though they appear to go beyond the limits indicated by the title, have none the less been deemed indispensable in their context. The justification for expressions and forms lies in the truth; it is not the converse that holds good. Truth is at the same time both single and infinite; hence the perfectly homogeneous diversity of its language.

This book is intended primarily for Western readers given the language in which it is written and the nature of its dialectic, but there are doubtless some Orientals, schooled in Western moulds—men who have perhaps lost sight of the solid grounds for faith in God and Tradition—who equally may be able to profit from it and in any case to understand that Tradition is not a childish and outmoded mythology but a science that is terribly real.

F.S.

God is the Light of the heavens and of the earth

QURAN

The first thing created by God was the Intellect

THE PROPHET

God did not distribute to His servants anything more to be esteemed than Intelligence

ALI

Contents

Chapter 1

Islam

ISLAM is the meeting between God as such and man as such.

God as such: that is to say God envisaged, not as He manifested Himself in a particular way at a particular time, but independently of history and inasmuch as He is what He is and also as by His nature He creates and reveals.

Man as such: that is to say man envisaged, not as a fallen being needing a miracle to save him, but as man, a theomorphic being endowed with an intelligence capable of conceiving of the Absolute and with a will capable of choosing what leads to the Absolute.

Premises of Islam

To say 'God' is to say also 'being', 'creating', 'revealing'; in other words it is to say 'Reality', 'Manifestation', 'Reintegration': to say 'man' is to say 'theomorphism', 'transcendent intelligence' and 'free will'. These are, in the author's meaning, the premises of the Islamic perspective, those which explain its every application and must never be lost sight of by anyone wanting to understand any particular aspect of Islam.

Man thus appears *a priori* as a dual receptacle made for the Absolute, and Islam comes to fill that receptacle, first with the truth of the Absolute and secondly with the law of the Absolute. Islam then is in essence a truth and a law—or the Truth and the Law—the former answering to the intelligence and the latter to the will. It is thus that Islam sets out to abolish both uncertainty and hesitation and, *a fortiori*, both error and sin; error in holding that the Absolute is not, or that it is relative, or that there are two Absolutes, or that the relative is absolute; sin places these errors on the level of the will or of action. These two doctrines of the Absolute and of man are respectively to be found in the two 'testimonies' of the Islamic faith, the first (*Lā ilaha illā 'Llāh*) concerning God and the second (*Muhammadun' rasūlu 'Llāh*) concerning the Prophet.

13

The idea of predestination, so strongly marked in Islam, does not do away with the idea of freedom. Man is subject to predestination because he is not God, but he is free because he is 'made in the image of God'. God alone is absolute freedom, but human freedom, despite its relativity—in the sense that it is 'relatively absolute'—is not something other than freedom any more than a feeble light is something other than light. To deny predestination would amount to pretending that God does not know events 'in advance' and so is not omniscient: *quod absit*.

To sum up: Islam confronts what is immutable in God with what is permanent in man. For 'exoteric' Christianity man is *a priori* will, or, more exactly, he is will corrupted; clearly the intelligence is not denied, but it is taken into consideration only as an aspect of will; man is will and in man will is intelligent; when the will is corrupted, so also is the intelligence corrupted in the sense that in no way could it set the will to rights. Therefore a divine intervention is needed: the sacrament. In the case of Islam, where man is considered as the intelligence and intelligence comes 'before' will, it is the content or direction of the intelligence which has sacramental efficacy: whoever accepts that the Transcendent Absolute alone is absolute and transcendent, and draws from this its consequences for the will, is saved. The Testimony of Faith—the *Shahādah*—determines the intelligence, and the Islamic Law—the *Sharī'ah*—determines the will; in Islamic esotericism—the *Tarīqah*—there are initiatic graces which serve as keys and underline our 'supernatural nature'. Once again, our salvation, its texture and its development, are prefigured by our theomorphism: since we are transcendent intelligence and free will it is this intelligence and this will, or it is transcendence and freedom, which will save us; God does no more than fill the receptacles man had emptied but not destroyed; to destroy them is not in man's power.

Again in the same way: only man has the gift of speech, because he alone among earthly creatures is 'made in the image of God' in a direct and integral manner; now, if it is this theomorphism which, thanks to a divine impulsion, brings about salvation or deliverance, speech has its part to play as well as intelligence and will. These last are indeed actualized by prayer, which is speech both divine and human, the act relating to the will and its content to intelligence; speech is as it were the immaterial, though sensory, body of our will and of our understanding; but speech is not necessarily exteriorized, for articulated thought also involves language. In Islam nothing is of greater importance than the canonical prayers (*ṣalāt*) directed towards the Kaaba and the 'mentioning of God' (*dhikru 'Llāh*) directed towards the heart; the speech of the Sufi is repeated in the universal prayer of humanity and even in the prayer, often inarticulate, of all beings.

What constitutes the originality of Islam is, not the discovery of the saving function of intelligence, will and speech—that function is clear enough and is known to every religion—but that it has made of this, within the framework of Semitic monotheism, the point of departure in a perspective of salvation and deliverance. Intelligence is identified with its content which brings salvation; it is nothing other than knowledge of Unity, or of the Absolute, and of the dependence of all things on it; in the same way the will is *el-islām*, in other words conformity to what is willed by God, or by the Absolute, on the one hand in respect of our earthly existence and our spiritual possibility, and on the other in respect both of man as such and of man in a collective sense; speech is communication with God and is essentially prayer and invocation. When seen from this angle Islam recalls to man not so much what he should know, do and say, as what intelligence, will and speech are, by very definition. The Revelation does not superadd new elements but unveils the fundamental nature of the receptacle.

This could also be expressed as follows: if man, being made in the image of God, is distinguished from the other creatures by having transcendent intelligence, free will and the gift of speech, then Islam is the religion of certainty, equilibrium and prayer, to take in their order the three deiform faculties. And thus we meet the triad traditional in Islam, that of *el-imān* (the 'Faith'), *el-islām* (the 'Law', literally, 'submission') and *el-ihsān* (the 'Way', literally, 'virtue'): now the essential means of this third element is the 'remembering of God' actualized through speech on the basis of the first two elements. From the metaphysical point of view which is here in question *el-imān* is certainty of the Absolute and of the attachment of all things to the Absolute; *el-islām*—and the Prophet inasmuch as he personifies Islam—is an equilibrium in terms of the Absolute and with the Absolute in view; and finally *el-ihsān* leads these first two back to their essences by the magic of sacred speech, inasmuch as this speech is the vehicle for both intelligence and will. The part thus played by man's aspects of theomorphism in what might be called fundamental and 'pre-theological' Islam is the more remarkable since Islamic doctrine, which emphasizes the transcendence of God and the incommensurability between Him and ourselves, is repugnant to analogies made for the advantage of man; thus Islam is far from relying explicitly and generally on man's quality of being a divine image, although the Quran bears testimony to it in the words: 'When I shall have formed him according to perfection and breathed into him a portion of My Spirit (*min-Rūhī*), fall down before him in prostration' (XV, 29 and XXXVIII, 72) and although the anthropomorphism of God in the Quran implies the theomorphism of man.

The doctrine of Islam hangs on two statements: first 'There is no divinity (or reality, or absolute) outside the only Divinity (or Reality, or Absolute)' (*Lā ilaha illā 'Llah*), and 'Muhammad (the "Glorified", the Perfect) is the Envoy (the mouthpiece, the intermediary, the manifestation, the symbol) of the Divinity' (*Muhammadun Rasūlu 'Llāh*); these are the first and the second 'Testimonies' (*Shahādat*) of the faith.

Here we are in the presence of two assertions, two certitudes, two levels of reality: the Absolute and the relative, Cause and effect, God and the world. Islam is the religion of certitude and equilibrium, as Christianity is the religion of love and sacrifice. By this we mean, not that religions have monopolies but that each lays stress on one or other aspect of truth. Islam seeks to implant certitude—its unitary faith stands forth as something manifestly clear without in any way renouncing mystery[1]— and is based on two axiomatic certainties, one concerning the Principle, which is both Being and Beyond-Being, and the other concerning manifestation, both formal and supraformal: thus it is a matter on the one hand of 'God'—or of 'The Godhead' in the sense in which Eckhart used that term—and on the other of 'Earth' and 'Heaven'. The first of these certainties is that 'God alone is' and the second that 'all things are attached to God'.[2]

---

[1] Mystery is as it were the inner infinity of certitude and the latter could not exhaust the former.

[2] These two relationships are also expressed in the following formula in the Quran: 'Verily we are God's (*innā lilLāhi*) and verily unto Him we return'

In other words: 'nothing is absolutely evident save the Absolute'; then, following on this truth: 'All manifestation, and so all that is relative, is attached to the Absolute.' The world is linked to God—or the relative to the Absolute—both in respect of its cause and of its end: the word 'Envoy', in the second *Shahādah*, therefore enunciates, first a causality and then a finality, the former particularly concerning the world and the second concerning man.[1]

All metaphysical truths are comprised in the first of these 'testimonies' and all eschatological truths in the second. But it could also be said that the first *Shahādah* is the formula of discernment or 'abstraction' (*tanzīh*) while the second is the formula of integration or 'analogy' (*tashbīh*): in the first *Shahādah* the word 'divinity' (*ilah*)—taken here in its ordinary current sense—designates the world inasmuch as it is unreal because God alone is real, while the name of the Prophet (*Muhammad*) in the second *Shahādah* designates the world inasmuch as it is real because nothing can be outside God; in certain respects all is He. Realizing the first *Shahādah* means first of all—'first of all' because this *Shahādah* includes the second in an eminent degree—becoming fully conscious that the Principle alone is real and that the world, though on its own level it 'exists', 'is not'; in one sense it therefore means realizing the universal void. Realizing the second *Shahādah* means first of all[2] becoming fully conscious that the world—or manifestation —is 'not other' than God or the Principle, since to the degree that it has reality it can only be that which alone 'is', or in other words it can only be divine; realizing this *Shahādah* thus means seeing God everywhere and everything in Him. 'He who has seen me', said the Prophet, 'has seen God'; now everything is the 'Prophet', on the one hand in respect of the perfection of

(*wa-innā ilayhi rāji'ūn*). The *Basmalah*, the formula: 'In the Name of God the infinitely Good, the ever Merciful' (*Bismi 'Llāhi 'Rrahmāni 'Rrahīm*) equally expresses the attachment of all things to the Principle.

[1] Or again, the cause or origin is in the word *rasūl* (Envoy) and the finality in the word *Muhammad* (Glorified). The *risālah* (the 'thing sent', the 'epistle', the Quran) 'came down' in the *laylat el-Qadr* (the 'night of the Power that is destiny') and Mohammad 'ascended' in the *laylat el-mi'rāj* (the 'night journey') thus prefiguring the end of man.

[2] 'First of all' meaning in this case that in the final analysis this *Shahādah*, being like the first a divine Word or 'Name', in the end actualizes the same knowledge as the first by virtue of the oneness of essence of the Word or Names of God.

existence and on the other in respect of the perfections of mode
or expression.[1]

If Islam merely sought to teach that there is only one God and
not two or more, it would have no persuasive force. In fact it
is characterized by persuasive ardour and this comes from the
fact that at root it teaches the reality of the Absolute and the
dependence of all things on the Absolute. Islam is the religion
of the Absolute as Christianity is the religion of love and of
miracle; but love and miracle also pertain to the Absolute and
express nothing other than an attitude It assumes in relation
to us.

If we go to the very root of things we are forced to observe
—setting aside any dogmatic question—that the basic reason
for the mutual lack of understanding between Christians and
Moslems lies in this: the Christian always sees before him his
will—the will that is as it were himself—and so is confronted by
an indeterminate vocational space into which he can plunge,
bringing into play his faith and his heroism; by contrast the
Islamic system of 'external' and clearly laid down prescriptions
seems to him the expression of a mediocrity ready to make all
kinds of concessions and incapable of any soaring flight: Moslem
virtue seems to him in theory—he is ignorant of its practice—
to be something artificial and empty. The outlook of the Moslem
is very different: he sees before him—before his intelligence
which chooses the One—not a space for the will such as would
seem to him a temptation to individualistic adventuring, but a
system of channels divinely predisposed for the equilibrium of
his volitive life, and this equilibrium, far from being an end in
itself as is supposed by the Christian, who is accustomed to a
more or less exclusive idealism of the will, is on the contrary
in the final analysis only a basis for escaping, in peace-giving
and liberating contemplation of the Immutable, from the
uncertainties and turbulence of the ego. To sum up: if the attitude of equilibrium which Islam seeks and realizes appears in
Christian eyes as a calculating mediocrity incapable of reaching

[1] In connection with Ibn Arabī a Spanish scholar has spoken of 'islam
cristianizado': this is to lose sight of the fact that the doctrine of the *Shaikh
el-akbar* was essentially Mohammadan and was in particular even a sort of
commentary on *Muhammadun rasūlu 'Llāh* in the meaning of the Vedantic
sayings: 'all things are Atma' and 'That art thou'.

the supernatural, the sacrificial idealism of Christianity is liable
to be misinterpreted by the Moslem as an individualism con-
temptuous of the divine gift of intelligence. If the objection is
raised that the average Moslem does not concern himself with
contemplation, the answer is that no more does the average
Christian bother himself with sacrifice; in the depths of his soul
every Christian nourishes an urge to sacrifice which will perhaps
never be actualized, and in the same way every Moslem has, by
reason of his faith, a predisposition to contemplation which will
perhaps never actually dawn in his heart. Apart from this
another objection might be made by some, who would say that
Christian and Moslem mysticism, far from being opposed types,
on the contrary present such striking analogies that one is felt
bound to conclude that there have been either unilateral or
reciprocal borrowings; to this the answer is that, if we suppose
the starting point of Sufis to have been the same as that of
Christian mystics, the question arises why they should have
remained Moslems and how they were able to endure being
Moslems; in reality they were saints not in spite of their religion
but through their religion. Far from being Christians in disguise
men like Al-Ḥallāj and Ibn 'Arabī on the contrary did no
more than carry the possibilities of Islam to their highest
point as their great forerunners had done. Despite certain
appearances, such as the absence of monasticism as a social
institution, Islam, which extols poverty, fasting, solitude
and silence, includes all the premises of a contemplative
asceticism.

When a Christian hears the word 'truth' he immediately
thinks of the fact that 'the Word was made flesh', whereas, when
a Moslem hears that word he thinks first of all that 'there is no
divinity apart from the sole Divinity' and will interpret this,
according to his level or knowledge, either literally or metaphysically. Christianity is founded on an 'event' and Islam on
'being', on 'the nature of things'; that which appears in Christianity as a unique fact, the Revelation, is seen in Islam as the
rhythmic manifestation of a principle. If, for Christians, the
truth is that Christ allowed himself to be crucified, for Moslems
—for whom the truth is that there is only one God—the cruci-
fixion of Christ is by its very nature such that it cannot be 'the
Truth', and the Moslem rejection of the cross is a way of expressing this. Moslem antihistoricism—and by analogy it could

be termed 'Platonic' or 'gnostic'—culminates in this rejection which is at root quite external and for some[1] even doubtful as to its intention.

The Fall too—and not only the Incarnation—is a unique 'event' deemed capable of determining 'being'—that of man—in a total manner. For Islam the fall of Adam is a necessary manifestation of evil but one which does not imply that evil can determine the true nature of man, since man cannot lose his theomorphism. In Christianity the divine 'action' appears in a way to have priority over the divine 'being' in the sense that the 'action' is reflected in the very definition of God. This way of looking at things may appear cursory, but there is here a very subtle distinction which cannot be neglected when comparing the two theologies in question.

The attitude of reserve adopted by Islam, not indeed towards miracles, but towards the Judaeo-Christian, and particularly the Christian, axiomatic assumption of miracles is explained by the predominance of the pole of 'intelligence' over the pole of 'existence': the Islamic outlook is based on what is spiritually evident, on the feeling of the Absolute, in conformity with the very nature of man which is in this case seen as a theomorphic intelligence and not as a will only waiting to be seduced in either a good or a bad sense, seduced, that is to say, by miracles or by temptations. If Islam, the last to appear in the series of great Revelations, is not founded on miracles—though of necessity admitting them, for otherwise it could not be a religion—this is also because Antichrist 'will lead many astray by his wonders'.[2] Now spiritual certainty (something at the very opposite pole from that 'turning upside down' produced by miracles), a certainty which Islam offers in the form of a penetrating unitary faith, an acute sense of the Absolute, is an element to which the devil has no access; he can imitate a miracle but not what is intellectually evident; he can imitate a phenomenon but not the Holy Spirit, except in the case of those who want to be deceived and have anyhow no sense either of the truth or of the sacred.

[1] As, for instance, for Abū Hātim, quoted by Louis Massignon in his *Le Christ dans les Evangiles selon Al-Ghazālī*.

[2] A Catholic writer of the end of last century could exclaim 'What we need is signs, concrete facts!' It is inconceivable that a Moslem should say such a thing; in Islam it would seem infidelity or even a call to the devil or to antichrist and anyhow a most blameworthy extravagance.

Allusion has already been made to the non-historical character of the Islamic perspective. This character explains, not only
its intention of being simply the repetition of a timeless reality
or a phase in a nameless rhythm, and so a 'reform'—in the
strictly orthodox and traditional meaning of the term, and
even in a transposed sense because an authentic Revelation is
inevitably spontaneous and comes only from God whatever the
appearance—but it also explains such Islamic ideas as that of
continual creation: were God not Creator at every moment the
world would pass away; since God is always Creator it is He who
intervenes in every phenomenon and there are no secondary
causes, no intermediate principles, no natural laws which can
come between God and the cosmic fact excepting only in the
case of man who, being the representative, the *imām*, of God on
earth, has those miraculous gifts, intelligence and freedom. But
in the final analysis not even these gifts escape the divine
determination; man freely chooses what God wills; he chooses
'freely' because God wills it thus, because God cannot fail to
manifest within the contingent order His absolute Freedom. So
our freedom is real, but with a reality that is illusory like the
relativity in which it is produced and in which it is a reflection
of That which is.

The fundamental difference between Christianity and Islam
after all shows up clearly in what Christians and Moslems
respectively detest: what is detestable for the Christian is, first,
the rejection of the divinity of Christ and of the Church and in
the second place morals less ascetic than his own, not to say lax;
as for the Moslem, he hates the rejection of Allah and of Islam
because the supreme Unity and its absoluteness and transcendence appear to him dazzlingly evident and majestic and because
for him Islam, the Law, is the divine Will and the logical
emanation, in the mode of equilibrium, of that Unity. Now the
divine Will—and here above all the whole difference shows
up—does not necessarily coincide with what involves sacrifice,
it may even in some cases combine the useful and the agreeable;
and so the Moslem will say: 'That is good which God wants',
not: 'What is painful is what God wants'; logically the Christian
is of the same opinion as the Moslem, but his sensibility and his
imagination lead him rather towards the second formulation.
In the climate of Islam the divine Will has in view in the first
place, not sacrifice and suffering as pledges of love, but the

deployment of the theomorphic intelligence (*min Rūḥī*, 'of My Spirit'), itself determined by the Immutable and thus including our being, otherwise there is 'hypocrisy' (*nifāq*) since to know is to be. In reality the apparent 'easiness' of Islam tends towards an equilibrium, as has already been pointed out, of which the sufficient reason is in the final analysis 'vertical' effort, contemplation, gnosis. In one sense what we must do is the opposite of what God does; in another sense we must act like Him: this is because on the one hand we are like God, since we exist, and on the other we are opposed to him since, in existing, we are separated from Him. For example, God is Love; so we ought to love because we are like Him; but, from another side, He judges and avenges, and this we cannot do because we are other than He; but as these positions are always approximate, morals can and must differ; there is always room in us—at any rate in principle—for a guilty love and a just vengeance. Here it is all a matter of accent and delimitation; the choice depends on a perspective which is not arbitrary (for then it would not be a perspective) but in conformity with the nature of things or with a particular aspect of that nature.

All the positions described above are founded on the dogmas or, in a deeper sense, on the metaphysical perspectives which they express, that is to say, on a certain 'point of view' as to the subject and on a certain 'aspect' as to the object. Seeing that Christianity is founded on the divinity of an earthly phenomenon—it is not in himself that Christ is earthly but in so far as he moves in space and time—Christianity is forced as a consequence to introduce relativity into the Absolute, or rather to consider the Absolute at a relative level, that of the Trinity;[1] since a particular 'relative' is considered as absolute the Absolute must have something of the relative, and since the Incarnation is a fact of the Divine Mercy or Love, God must be envisaged at the outset in this aspect and man in the corres-

---

[1] To speak of distinction is to speak of relativity. The very term 'trinitarian relationships' proves that the point of view adopted—providentially and necessarily adopted—stands at the level proper to all *bhakti*. Gnosis goes beyond this level in attributing absoluteness to the 'Godhead' in the Eckhartian sense, or to the 'Father' when the Trinity is envisaged 'vertically', in which case the 'Son' corresponds to Being—the first relativity 'in the Absolute'—and the Holy Spirit to Act.

ponding aspect of will and affection; and equally the spiritual path must be a reality of love. The Christian emphasis on the will is the counterpart of the Christian conception of the Absolute and, if the expression is permissible, this in turn is as if determined by the 'historicity' of God.

Analogously, seeing that Islam is founded on the absoluteness of God, it is forced as a consequence—since by its form it is a Semitic dogmatism[1]—to exclude all that is earthly from the Absolute and so must, at least on the level of words, deny the divinity of Christ; it is not obliged to deny that in a secondary manner the relative is in God for inevitably it admits the divine attributes, otherwise it would be denying the totality of God and all possibility of connection between God and the world; but it has to deny any directly divine character outside the single Principle. The Sufis are the first to recognize that nothing can stand outside the supreme Reality, for to say that Unity excludes everything amounts to saying that from another point of view—that of the reality of the world—it includes everything; but this truth is not susceptible of dogmatic formulation, though it is logically included in the *Lā ilaha illā 'Llāh*.

When the Quran affirms that the Messiah is not God it means he is not 'a god' other than God, or that he is not God *qua* the earthly Messiah;[2] and when the Quran rejects the dogma of the Trinity it means there is no triad in 'God as such', that is, in the Absolute, which is beyond all distinctions. Finally, when the Quran appears to deny the death of Christ, it can be understood to mean that in reality Jesus vanquished death, whereas the Jews believed they had killed the Christ in his very essence;[3] here the truth of the symbol prevails over the truth of the fact in the sense that a spiritual negation takes the form of a material

[1] Dogmatism is characterized by the fact that it attributes an absolute scope and an exclusive sense to a particular 'point of view' or 'aspect'. In pure metaphysics all conceptual antinomies are resolved in the total truth, something which must not be confused with a levelling out of real oppositions by denying them.

[2] In Christian terms: human nature is not divine nature. If Islam insists on this, as it does, in one particular way and not in some other that is because of its angle of vision.

[3] The Quran says: 'Say not of those that have been slain in the way of God that they are dead; say that they are living, though ye are not aware of it.' See also *Gnosis* by F. Schuon, Murray, 1959.

negation;[1] but, from another angle, by this negation, or apparent negation, Islam eliminates the way of Christ in what concerns itself, and it is logical that it should do this since its own way is different and it has no need to claim those means of grace which are proper to Christianity.

On the plane of total truth, which includes all possible points of view, aspects and modes, any recourse to reason alone is evidently useless: consequently it is vain to adduce against some dogma of a 'foreign' religion that an error denounced by reason cannot become a truth on another level, for that is to forget that the reason works in an indirect way, or by reflections, and that its axioms are inadequate in so far as it trespasses on the ground of pure intellect. Reason is formal by its nature and formalistic in its operations; it proceeds by 'coagulations', by alternatives and by exclusions—or, it can be said, by partial truths. It is not, like pure intellect, formless and "fluid' light; true, it derives its implacability, or its validity in general, from the intellect, but it touches on essences only through drawing conclusions, not by direct vision; it is indispensable for verbal formulation but it does not involve immediate knowledge.

In Christianity the line of demarcation between the relative and the Absolute passes through Christ; in Islam it separates the world from God, or even—in the case of esotericism—the divine attributes from the Essence, a difference explained by the fact that exotericism has always to start from the relative while esotericism starts from the Absolute to which it gives a more strict, and even the strictest possible meaning. In Sufism it is also said that the divine attributes are predicated as such only in respect of the world and that in themselves they are

---

[1] The same remark applies to Christianity as when, for instance, the saints of the Old Testament—even Enoch, Abraham, Moses and Elias—are held to have remained shut out from Heaven till the 'descent into Hell' of Christ; none the less, before that descent, Christ appeared between Moses and Elias in the light of the transfiguration, and in a parable mentioned 'the bosom of Abraham'; clearly these facts are capable of various interpretations, but the Christian concepts are none the less incompatible with the Jewish tradition. What justifies them is their spiritual symbolism and thus their truth: salvation must of necessity come through the Logos which, though manifested in time in a particular form, is beyond the limitations of a temporal condition. Notice equally the seeming contradiction between St John the Baptist denying that he was Elias and Christ affirming the contrary: had this contradiction, which is resolved by the difference in the relationship envisaged, been between one religion and another, it would have been exploited to the uttermost on the pretext that 'God cannot contradict Himself'.

indistinct and ineffable: so one cannot say of God that He is, in an absolute sense, 'merciful' or 'avenger', leaving aside for the moment that He is merciful 'before' being avenger; as for the attributes of the Essence such as 'holiness' or 'wisdom' they are only actualized as distinctions in respect of our distinctive mind, and they are so without on that account losing anything, in their own being, of their infinite reality, quite the contrary.

To say that the Islamic perspective is possible amounts to saying that it is necessary and consequently cannot fail to be; it is required by its providential human receptacles. The different perspectives as such have however no absolute quality, Truth being one; in the eyes of God their differences are relative and the values of any one are always to be found in others in some manner. There is not only a Christianity of 'warmth', of emotional love, of sacrificial activity, but, framed within this, there is also a Christianity of 'light', of gnosis, of pure contemplation, of 'peace', and in the same way the Islam that is 'dry'— whether legalistically or metaphysically—encloses an Islam that is 'moist',[1] an Islam, that is to say, much preoccupied with beauty, with love and with sacrifice. This must needs be so because of the unity, not only of the Truth, but also of man, a unity no doubt relative, since differences do exist, but nevertheless sufficiently real to allow of, or to impose, the reciprocity —or the spiritual ubiquity—in question.

Here there is a point to be touched on, the question of Moslem morality. If we want to understand certain seeming contradictions in that morality we must take into account the fact that Islam distinguishes between man as such and collective man, the latter appearing as a new creature subject in a certain degree, but no further, to the law of natural selection. This is to say that Islam puts everything in its proper place and treats it according to its own nature; collective man it envisages, not through the distorting perspective of a mystical idealism which is in fact inapplicable, but taking account of the natural laws which regulate each order and are, within the limits of each order, willed by God. Islam is the perspective of certainty and of the nature of things rather than of miracles and idealist improvisation. This is said, not with any underlying intention

[1] The terms are used here in an alchemical sense.

of indirectly criticizing Christianity, which is what it should be, but in order better to bring out the intention and justification of the Islamic perspective.

If we start with the idea that esotericism by definition considers first of all the being of things and not becoming or our situation in relation to our will, then for the Christian gnostic it is Christ who is the being of things, this 'Word from which all things were made and without which nothing was made'. The Peace of Christ is from this point of view the repose of the intellect in 'that which is'.

If there is a clear separation in Islam between man as such[1] and collective man, these two realities are none the less profoundly linked together, given that the collectivity is an aspect of man—no man can be born without a family—and that conversely society is a multiplication of individuals. It follows from this interdependence or reciprocity that anything that is done with a view to the collectivity, such as the tithe for the poor or the holy war, has a spiritual value for the individual and conversely; this converse relationship is the more true because the individual comes before the collectivity, all men being descended from Adam and not Adam from men.

What has just been said explains why the Moslem does not, like the Buddhist and the Hindu, abandon external rites in following some particular spiritual method which can compensate for them, or because he has attained a spiritual level of a nature to authorize such abandonment.[2] A particular

[1] The expression 'single man' is not used here because it would have the disadvantage of defining man in terms of the collectivity and not starting from God. The distinction made is not between one man and several men but between the human person and society.

[2] The principle of this abandonment of the rites of the generality is none the less known and is sometimes manifested, otherwise Ibn Hanbal would not have reproached Sufis with developing meditation to the detriment of the prayers and in short with pretentions to freeing themselves from the obligations of the law. In fact a distinction is drawn between dervishes who are 'travellers' (towards God; *sālikūn*) and those who are 'attracted' (by God; *majādhīb*); those in the first category form the vast majority and do obey the Law, whereas those in the second more or less dispense with it and are not much molested because they are generally held to be half mad and so worthy of pity, sometimes of fear or even of veneration. Among Sufis in Indonesia cases of the abandoning of rites in favour of prayer of the heart alone seem not to be rare; consciousness of the Divine Unity is then deemed a universal prayer which gives dispensation from the canonical prayers; the supreme knowledge is held to exclude the 'polytheistic' (*mushrik*) multiplicity of the rites, the Absolute being without duality. In Islam in general there always seems to have existed—quite apart

26

saint may no longer have need of the canonical prayers since he finds himself in a state of being steeped in prayer, in a state of 'intoxication'[1]—none the less he continues to accomplish the prayers in order to pray with and for all and in order that all may pray in him. He is the incarnation of that 'mystical Body' which every believing community constitutes, or, from another point of view, he incarnates the Law, the tradition and prayer as such. Inasmuch as he is a social being he should preach by his example and, inasmuch as he is individual man, permit what is human to be realized and in some sense renewed through him.

The metaphysical transparency of things and the contemplativity answering to it mean that sexuality (within the framework of its traditional legitimacy, which is one of psychological and social equilibrium) can take on a meritorious character, as the existence of this framework indeed already shows. In other words it is not only the enjoyment which counts —leaving aside the care to preserve the species—for sexuality also has its qualitative content, its symbolism which is both objective and something lived. The basis of Moslem morality is always in biological reality and not in an idealism contrary to collective possibilities and to the undeniable rights of natural laws; but this reality, while forming the basis of our animal and collective life, has no absolute quality since we are semi-celestial beings; it can always be neutralized on the level of our personal liberty, though never abolished on that of our social

---

from the very special distinction between *sālikūn* and *majādhib*—an external division between those Sufis who were 'nomian' and those who were anti-nomian, the former being attached to the Law by virtue of its symbolism and its opportuneness and the latter detached from the Law by virtue of the supremacy of the heart (*Qalb*) and direct knowledge (*ma'rifah*). Jalāl ed-Dīn Rūmī says in his Mathnāwī: 'The lovers of rites form one class and those whose hearts are afire with love form another', a remark addressed to Sufis alone, as is shown by his reference to the 'essence of certainty' (*'ayn al-yaqīn*), and clearly not including any suggestion of a systematic alternative, as is proved by the life of Jalāl ed-Dīn himself; no 'free-thinking' could draw support from it. Finally it may be noted that according to Al-Junayd 'he who realizes union' (*muwahhid*) should observe 'sobriety' (*sahw*) and keep himself from 'intoxication' (*sukr*) just as much as from 'libertinism' (*ibāhiyah*).

[1] The Quran says: 'Do not go to the prayer in a state of drunkenness', and this can be understood in a higher and positive sense; the Sufi who enjoys a 'station' (*maqām*) of bliss, or even merely the *dhākir* (the man given up to *dhikr*, the Islamic equivalent of the Hindu *japa*) could, considering his secret prayer to be like a 'wine' (*khamr*), in principle abstain from the general prayers; 'in principle' for in fact the care for equilibrium and solidarity, so marked in Islam, make the balance tend in the other direction.

existence.[1] What has just been said of sexuality applies by
analogy, but only in respect of merit, to food: as in the case of
all religions, overeating is a sin, but to eat in due measure and
with gratitude to God is, in Islam, not only not a sin but a
positively meritorious action. The analogy is not, however,
total, for in a well-known *hadīth*, the Prophet said he 'loved
women', not that he loved 'food'. Here the love of woman is
connected with nobility and generosity, not to mention
its purely contemplative symbolism which goes far beyond
this.

Islam is often reproached with having propagated its faith
by the sword; what is overlooked is, first, that persuasion played
a much greater part than war in the expansion of Islam as a
whole, and, secondly, that only polytheists and idolators could
be compelled to embrace the new religion,[2] thirdly, that the God
of the Old Testament is no less a warrior than the God of the
Quran, quite the opposite, and, fourthly, that Christianity also
made use of the sword from the time of Constantine's appearance
on the scene. The question to be put here is simply the following:
is it possible for force to be used with the aim of affirming and
diffusing a vital truth? Beyond doubt the answer must be in
the affirmative, for experience proves that we must at times do
violence to irresponsible people in their own interest. Now,
since this possibility exists it cannot fail to be manifested in
appropriate conditions,[3] exactly as in the case of the opposite
possibility of victory through the force inherent in truth itself;
it is the inner or outer nature of things which determines the
choice between two possibilities. On the one hand the end
sanctifies the means, and on the other hand the means may
profane the end, which signifies that the means must be found

[1] Many Hindu saints have disregarded caste, but none have dreamt of
abolishing it. To the question whether there are two moralities, one for individuals and the other for the state, our reply is affirmative, subject to the
reservation that the one can always extend to the domain of the other according
to external or internal circumstances. Never in any circumstances is it permissible for the intention 'not to resist evil' to become complicity, betrayal or
suicide.

[2] This attitude ceased in relation to Hindus, at any rate in large measure,
once the Moslems had grasped that Hinduism was not equivalent to the
paganism of the Arabs; Hindus were in that case assimilated to the 'people of
the Book' (*ahl al-Kitāb*), that is to the Monotheists of the Western Semitic
traditions.

[3] Christ, in using violence against the money-changers in the temple, showed
that this attitude could not be excluded.

prefigured in the divine nature; thus the right of the stronger is prefigured in the 'jungle' to which beyond question we belong to a certain degree and when regarded as collectivities; but in that 'jungle' no example can be found of any right to perfidy and baseness and, even if such characteristics were to be found there, our human dignity would forbid us to participate in them. The harshness of certain biological laws must never be confused with that infamy of which man alone is capable through his perverted theomorphism.[1]

From a certain point of view it can be said that Islam has two dimensions, the 'horizontal' dimension of the will, and the 'vertical' dimension of the intelligence: the former we shall term 'equilibrium',[2] and the latter 'union'. Islam is in essence equilibrium and union; it does not primarily sublimate the will by sacrifice, but neutralizes it by the Law, while at the same

---

[1] 'We see Moslem and Catholic princes not only in alliance when it is a question of breaking the power of a dangerous fellow-religionist, but also generously helping one another to conquer disorders and revolts. Not without some shaking of the head will the reader learn that in one of the battles for the Caliphate of Cordova, in A.D. 1010 it was Catalan forces who saved the situation and that on this field three bishops gave their lives for the "Prince of the Faithful" . . . Al-Manṣûr had in his company several Counts, who had joined him with their troops, and there was nothing exceptional in the presence of Christian guards at the court of Andalusia. . . . When an enemy territory was conquered the religious convictions of the population were respected as much as possible; let us here only recall that Al-Manṣûr—in general a man of few scruples—took pains, at the assault on Santiago, to protect against any profanation the church containing the tomb of the Apostle, and that in many other cases the Caliphs seized the chance to show their respect for the sacred objects of the enemy: in similar circumstances the Christians adopted a like attitude. For centuries Islam was respected in the reconquered countries, and it was only in the XVI century that . . . it came to be systematically persecuted and exterminated at the instigation of a fanatical clergy who had become overpowerful. In contrast to this through the whole of the Middle Ages tolerance of this foreign conviction and respect for the feelings of the enemy accompanied incessant fighting between Moors and Christians and greatly softened the rigours and miseries of the warfare, giving to the battles a character as chivalrous as possible. . . . Despite the gulf between them in the matter of language this respect for the adversary and the high esteem of his virtues became a common national bond coupled as they were with the understanding shown in the poetry of both sides of the feelings of the other; indeed this poetry eloquently testifies to the love or friendship often uniting Moslems and Christians despite every obstacle.' (Ernst Kühnel: *Maurische Kunst*, Berlin, 1924.)

[2] Disequilibrium also includes a positive meaning, but only indirectly; every holy war is a disequilibrium. Certain sayings of Christ can be interpreted as instituting disequilibrium with a view to union, such as 'Think not that I am come to send peace on earth'; God alone will then restore the equilibrium.

time laying stress on contemplation. The dimensions of equilibrium and union, the horizontal and the vertical, concern both man as such and the community; there is not identity here assuredly, but there is a solidarity which makes society participate in its own way and according to its own possibilities in the individual's way to Union, and the converse is also true. One of the most important modes of realizing equilibrium is precisely an accord between the sacred Law relating to man as such and the law relating to society. Empirically, Christianity had through force of circumstances also reached this position, but it allowed certain 'fissures' to remain and did not lay stress in the first instance either on the divergence of the two human planes or, consequently, on the need to harmonize them. Let us repeat that Islam is an equilibrium determined by the Absolute and disposed with a view to the Absolute; this equilibrium, like the rhythm which in Islam is realized ritually through the canonical prayers following the sun's progress and 'mythologically' through the retrospective series of divine 'Messengers' and of revealed 'Books', is the participation of the many in the One or of the conditioned in the Unconditioned; without equilibrium we do not, on the basis of this perspective, find the centre, and apart from the centre no ascent and no union is possible. If equilibrium concerns the 'centre', rhythm is more particularly related to the 'origin' envisaged as the qualitative root of things.

Like all traditional civilizations Islam is a 'space', not a 'time', for Islam 'time' is only the corruption of this 'space'. 'No period will come', predicted the Prophet, 'which will not be worse than the period before it.' The 'space', this unvarying tradition—unvarying apart from the spreading and diversification of forms at the time of the initial elaboration of the tradition—surrounds Moslem humanity as a symbol, like the physical world which unvaryingly and imperceptibly nourishes us with its symbolism; it is normal for humanity to live in a symbol, which is a pointer towards heaven, an opening towards the Infinite. As for modern science it has pierced the protecting frontiers of this symbol and by so doing destroyed the symbol itself; it has thus abolished this pointer, this opening, even as the modern world in general breaks through the space-symbols constituted by traditional civilizations; what it terms 'stagnation' and 'sterility' is really the homogeneity and continuity of

symbols

the symbol.[1] When a still authentic Moslem says to the pro-
tagonists of progress; 'All that remains for you to do now is to
abolish death', or when he asks: 'Can you prevent the sun from
setting or compel it to rise?' he exactly expresses what lies at
the root of Islamic 'sterility'; it is a marvellous sense of relativity
and, what amounts to the same thing a sense of the Absolute
dominating his whole life.

In order to understand traditional civilizations in general and
Islam in particular it is also necessary to take account of the
fact that the human form is for them, not the common man
deeply immersed in illusion, but the saint, detached from the
world and attached to God; he alone is entirely 'normal' and he
alone enjoys on this account 'full right' to exist; it is this outlook which gives them a certain lack of sensibility in relation to
human nature as such. As this human nature is largely insensible
in relation to the Sovereign Good it should at least have fear
of that Good, in so far as it does not have love.

[margin handwritten note: Each MAN, Saintly "full right" to exist]

In the life of a people there are as it were two halves; one
constitutes the play of its earthly existence, the other its relationship with the Absolute. Now what determines the value of
a people or of a civilization is not the literal form of its earthly
dream—for here everything is only a symbol—but its capacity
to 'feel' the Absolute and, in the case of specially privileged
souls, to reach the Absolute. So it is completely illusory to set
aside this 'absolute' dimension and evaluate a human world
according to earthly criteria, as by comparing one civilization
materially with another. The gap of some thousands of years
separating the stone age of the Red Indians from the material
and literary refinements of the white man counts for nothing
compared with the contemplative intelligence and the virtues,
which alone impart value to man and alone make up his per-

[1] 'Neither India nor the Pythagoreans practised modern science, and to
isolate where they are concerned the elements of rational technique reminiscent
of our science from the metaphysical elements which bear no resemblance to
it is an arbitrary and violent operation contrary to real objectivity. When
Plato is decanted in this way he retains no more than an anecdotal interest,
whereas his whole doctrine aims at installing man in the supra-temporal and
supradiscursive life of thought of which both mathematics and the sensory
world can be symbols. If, then, peoples have been able to do without our
autonomous science for thousands of years and in every climate, it is because
this science is not necessary; if it has appeared as a phenomenon of civilization
suddenly and in a single place, that is to show its essentially contingent
nature.' (Fernand Brunner: *Science et Réalité*, Paris, 1954.)

manent reality, or that something which enables us to evaluate him in a real manner, as it were in the sight of the Creator. To believe that some men are 'lagging behind' us because their earthly dream takes on modes more 'rudimentary' than our own—modes which are often for the same reason more sincere—is far more naïve than to believe the earth is flat or a volcano is a god; the most naïve of all attitudes is surely to regard the dream as something absolute and to sacrifice to it all substantial values, forgetting that what is 'serious' only starts beyond its level, or rather that, if there is anything 'serious' in this world, it is so in terms of that which lies beyond it.

Modern civilization as a type of thought or culture is often contrasted with the traditional civilizations, but it is forgotten that modern thought, or the culture engendering it, is only an indeterminate flux, which in a sense cannot be defined positively since it lacks any principle that is real and so related to the Immutable. Modern thought is not in any definitive sense one doctrine among others; it is now the result of a particular phase of its own unfolding and will become what materialistic and experimental science or machines make it; no longer is it human intellect but machines—or physics, or chemistry or biology—which decide what man is, what intelligence is, what truth is. Under these conditions man's mind more and more depends on the 'climate' produced by its own creations: man no longer knows how to judge as a man, in function, that is to say, of an absolute which is the very substance of the intelligence; losing himself in a relativism that leads nowhere he lets himself be judged, determined and classified by the contingencies of science and technology; no longer able to escape from the dizzy fatality they impose on him and unwilling to admit his mistake[1] the only course left to him is to abdicate his human dignity and freedom. It is then science and machines which in their turn create man and, if such an expression may be ventured, they also 'create God'[2] for the void thus left by

[1] Here there is a kind of perversion of the instinct of self-preservation, a need to consolidate error in order to have an easy conscience.

[2] The speculations of Teilhard de Chardin provide a striking example of a theology that has succumbed to microscopes and telescopes, to machines and to their philosophical and social consequences, a 'fall' that would have been unthinkable had there been here the slightest direct intellective knowledge of the immaterial realities. The 'inhuman' side of the doctrine in question is highly significant.

dethroning God cannot remain empty, the reality of God and his imprint in human nature require a usurper of divinity, a false absolute which can fill the nothingness of an intelligence robbed of its substance. There is a great deal of talk in these days about 'humanism', talk which ignores the fact that, once man abandons to matter, to machines, to quantitative knowledge his own prerogative he ceases to be truly 'human'. What is most totally human is what gives man the best chances for the beyond and, by the same token, what also most deeply corresponds to his nature.

Def. of Human (?)

When people talk about 'civilization' they generally attribute a qualitative meaning to the term, but really civilization only represents a value provided it is supra-human in origin and implies for the 'civilized' man a sense of the sacred: only a people who really have this sense and draw their life from it are truly civilized. If it is objected that this reservation does not take account of the whole meaning of the term and that it is possible to conceive of a world that is 'civilized' though having no religion, the answer is that in this case the 'civilization' is devoid of value, or rather—since there is no legitimate choice between the sacred and other things—that it is the most mortal of aberrations. A sense of the sacred is fundamental for every civilization because fundamental for man; the sacred—that which is immutable, inviolable and so infinitely majestic—is in the very substance of our spirit and of our existence. The world is sick because men live beneath themselves; the error of modern man is that he wants to reform the world without having either the will or the power to reform man, and this flagrant contradiction, this attempt to make a better world on the basis of a worsened humanity, can only end in the abolition even of what is human, and consequently the abolition of happiness too. Reforming man means binding him again to Heaven, re-establishing the broken link, it means plucking him from the kingdom of the passions, from the cult of matter, quantity and cunning, and re-integrating him into the world of the spirit and serenity—even, it might be said, into the world of his own sufficient reason.

The SACRED

How to reform MAN

In this order of ideas, and because there are so-called Moslems who do not hesitate to describe Islam as 'pre-civilization', a distinction must here be drawn between a 'fall', a 'decadence', a 'degeneration' and a 'deviation'. The whole of humanity is

33

'fallen' through the loss of Eden and also, more particularly, because it is involved in the 'iron age'; some civilizations, such as most traditional worlds of the East at the time of the expansion of the West, can be called 'decadent';[1] a great many savage tribes are 'degenerate' according to the degree of their barbarism; as for modern civilization it has 'deviated' and the deviation is itself more and more combined with a real decadence that is especially palpable in literature and art. If Islam is to be called 'pre-civilization' this could well be termed a 'post-civilization'.

Here a question arises, somewhat aside from the general thesis of this book but none the less linked with it since in speaking of Islam it is necessary to speak of tradition and in dealing with tradition it must be explained what it is not. The question is this: what is the practical significance of the requirement, so often formulated today, that religion ought to be orientated towards social problems? Quite simply it means that religion ought to be orientated towards machines, or, to put it bluntly, that theology ought to become the handmaid of industry. No doubt there have always been social problems resulting from abuses which have arisen on the one hand from the fall of humanity and on the other from the existence of very large collectivities containing unequal groupings; but in the Middle Ages (a period deemed far from ideal by the men of that time) and even much later the artisan drew a large measure of happiness from his work, which was still human, and from surroundings which were still in conformity with an ethnic and spiritual genius. Whatever may have been the situation at that time, today the modern workman exists and the truth does concern him: he should understand, first of all that there is no question of recognizing in the wholly factitious quality of 'worker' a character belonging to an intrinsically human category, since the men who are in fact workers may belong to any natural category whatsoever; secondly he should understand that every external situation is only relative, man always

---

[1] It was not, however, this decadence which rendered them open to colonization, but on the contrary their normal character, which excluded 'technical progress'; Japan, which was hardly decadent, was no more successful in resisting the first assault of Western arms than other countries. We hasten to add that in these days the old opposition between West and East is hardly anywhere valid in the political field or is valid only within nations; externally there are only variants of the modern spirit which oppose one another.

remaining man, and that truth and spiritual life can adapt themselves, thanks to their universality and imperative character, to any situation whatever so that the so-called 'problem of the industrial worker' is at bottom quite simply the problem of man placed in those particular circumstances, and so still the problem of man as such; finally he should understand that truth does not require of any man that he should allow himself to be oppressed, when such a situation arises, by forces which themselves also only serve machines, any more than it allows man to base his demands on envy, which in any case could not be the measure of man's needs. It must be added that, if all men obeyed the profound law inscribed in the human condition, there would be no more social or even general human problems; leaving aside the question whether mankind can be reformed—and in fact this is impossible—one should in any case reform oneself and never believe that inner realities are of no importance for the equilibrium of the world. It is just as important to beware of a chimerical optimism as of despair; the former is contrary to the ephemeral reality of the world we live in and the latter to the eternal reality we already bear in ourselves, which alone makes intelligible our human and earthly condition.

According to an Arab proverb which reflects the Moslem's attitude to life, slowness comes from God and haste from Satan,[1] and this leads to the following reflection: as machines devour time modern man is always in a hurry, and, as this perpetual lack of time creates in him reflexes of haste and superficiality, modern man mistakes these reflexes—which compensate corresponding forms of disequilibrium—for marks of superiority and in his heart despises the men of old with their 'idyllic' habits, and especially the old-style Oriental with his slow gait and his turban, which takes so long to wind on. Having no experience of it people today cannot imagine what made up the qualitative content of traditional 'leisureliness' nor the manner of 'dreaming' of men of olden days; instead they content themselves with caricature, which is much simpler and is moreover demanded by an illusory instinct of self-preservation. If the outlook of today is so largely determined by social preoccupations with an evident material basis, it is not merely because of the social consequences of mechanization and the human

[1] *Festina lente*, said the Latin proverb.

conditions this engenders, but also because of the absence of any contemplative atmosphere such as is essential to the welfare of man whatever his 'standard of living', to use an expression as barbarous as it is common. Any contemplative attitude is today labelled 'escapism'—in German *Weltflucht*—and this includes any refusal to situate total truth and the meaning of life in external agitation. A hypocritically utilitarian attachment to the world is dignified as 'responsibilities' and people hasten to ignore the fact that flight—even supposing it was only a question of an escape—is not always a wrong attitude.

Reference has been made to the turban when speaking of the slowness of traditional rhythms,[1] and on this point we must pause for reflection. The association of ideas between the turban and Islam is far from fortuitous: 'The turban', said the Prophet, 'is a frontier between faith and unbelief', and he also said: 'My community shall not fall away so long as they wear the turban.' The following *ahadīth* are also quoted in this context: 'At the Day of Judgment a man shall receive a light for each turn of the turban (*kawrah*) round his head'; 'Wear turbans, for thus you will gain in generosity.' The point we wish to make is that the turban is deemed to give the believer a sort of gravity, consecration and majestic humility;[2] it puts him apart from chaotic and dissipated creatures—the *dāllūn*, the 'strayers', of the *Fātihah*—fixing him on a divine axis—*es-sirat el-mustaqīm*, the 'straight path' of the same prayer—and thus destines him for contemplation; in brief the turban is like a celestial counterpoise to all that is profane and empty. Since it is the head, the brain, which is for us the plane of our choice between true and false, durable and ephemeral, real and illusory, weighty and futile, it is the head which should also bear the mark of this choice; the material symbol is deemed to

---

[1] This slowness does not exclude speed when speed follows from the natural properties of things or results naturally from the circumstances, showing it then to be in accord with the corresponding spiritual symbolisms and attitudes. It is in the nature of a horse to be able to gallop and an Arab 'fantasia' is executed at high speed; a sword stroke must be of lightning speed and so must decisions at moments of danger. The ablution before prayer must be made quickly.

[2] In Islam the angels and all the prophets are represented as wearing turbans, sometimes of differing colours according to the symbolism.

reinforce the spiritual consciousness, and this is, moreover, true of every religious head-dress and even of every liturgical vestment or merely traditional dress. The turban so to speak envelops man's thinking, always so prone to dissipation, forgetfulness and infidelity; it recalls the sacred imprisoning of his passional nature prone to flee from God.[1] It is the function of the Quranic Law to re-establish a primordial equilibrium that was lost; hence the *hadīth*: 'Wear turbans and thus distinguish yourselves from the peoples (lacking in equilibrium) who came before you.'

Hatred of the turban, like hatred of the romantic, or the picturesque or what belongs to folk-lore, is explained by the fact that the 'romantic' worlds are precisely those in which God is still probable; when people want to get rid of Heaven it is logical to start by creating an atmosphere in which spiritual things appear out of place; in order to be able to declare successfully that God is unreal they have to construct around man a false reality, a reality that is inevitably inhuman because only the inhuman can exclude God. What is involved is a falsification of the imagination and so its destruction; modern mentality implies the most prodigious lack of imagination imaginable.

pretty vast state-ments.

At this point something must be said about the Moslem woman's veil. Islam makes a sharp separation between the world of man and that of woman, between the community as a whole and the family which is its kernel, between the street and the home, just as it sharply separates society and the individual or exotericism and esotericism. The home, and the woman who is its incarnation, are regarded as having an inviolable, and so a sacred, character. Woman even in a certain manner incarnates esotericism by reason of certain aspects of her nature and function; 'esoteric truth', the *haqīqah*, is 'felt' as a 'feminine' reality, and the same is true of *barakah*. Moreover the veil and the seclusion of woman are connected with the final cyclic phase in which we live—and they present a certain analogy with the forbidding of wine and the veiling of the mysteries.

The differences between traditional worlds are not limited to differences of perspective and of dogma, there are also differ-

---

[1] When St Vincent de Paul designed the head-dress of the Sisters of Charity he intended to give them an air reminiscent of monastic isolation.

ences of temperament and of taste: thus the European temperament does not readily tolerate exaggeration as a mode of
expression whereas for the Oriental hyperbole is a way of
bringing out an idea or an intention, of marking the sublime or
of expressing what cannot be described, such as the appearing
of an angel or the radiance of a saint. An Occidental attaches
importance to factual exactitude, but his lack of intuition
regarding the 'immutable essences' (ayān thābitah) counter-
balances this, greatly diminishing the range of his spirit of
observation; an Oriental on the contrary has a sense of the
metaphysical transparency of things but is apt to neglect the
literal aspect of earthly facts; for him the symbol is more
important than the experience.

This symbolical hyperbole is in part explained by the following principle: between a form and its content there is not only
analogy, but also opposition; if the form, or the expression,
must normally be in the likeness of what it transmits, it can
also find itself 'neglected' in favour of the pure content by
reason of the distance separating 'external' from 'internal', or
it may be as it were 'broken' by the super-abundance of the
content. The man who is only attached to the 'inward' may
have no awareness of outer forms, or the converse may be true
of him; one man will appear sublime because he is a saint and
another pitiful for the same reason; and what is true of man is
true also of his speech and writings. Sometimes the price of
profundity or sublimity is a lack of critical sense in relation to
appearances; this assuredly does not mean that such must be
the case, for here is but a paradoxical possibility; in other
words, when pious exaggeration arises from an overflowing of
perception and of sincerity, it has the 'right' not to note the
fact that its draughtsmanship is poor and it would be ungrate-
ful and out of proportion to reproach it for this. Piety as well as
truthfulness requires us to see the excellence of the intention
and not the weakness of expression where such an alternative
presents itself.

5
pillars

The pillars (arkān) of Islam are these: the double testimony
of faith (the shahādatān), the canonical prayer repeated five
times a day (the salāt), the fast of Ramadan (siyām, sawm), the
tithe (zakāt), the pilgrimage (the hajj); to these is sometimes
added the holy war (the jihād), which has a more or less acci-

dental character since it depends on circumstances;[1] as for the
ablution (the *wudhū* or the *ghusl* according to circumstances),
it is not mentioned separately for it is a condition of the prayer.
As we have already seen the *shahādah* indicates in the final
analysis—and it is the most universal meaning which interests us
here—discernment between the Real and the unreal and then,
in the second part, the attaching of the world to God in respect
both of its origin and of its end, for to look on things separately
from God is already unbelief (*nifāq*, *shirk* or *kufr* as the case
may be). The prayer integrates man into the rhythm of universal adoration and—through the ritual orientation of the
prayer towards the *Kaaba*—into its centripetal order; the
ablution preceding the prayer brings man back in virtuality to
the primordial state and in a certain manner to pure Being. The
fast cuts man off from the continual and devouring flux of carnal
life, introducing into our flesh a kind of death and purification;[2]
the alms vanquish egoism and avarice and actualize the
solidarity of all creatures, for alms are a fasting of the soul, even
as the fast proper is an almsgiving of the body. The pilgrimage
is a pre-figuration of the inward journey towards the *kaaba* of
the heart and purifies the community, just as the circulation of
the blood, passing through the heart, purifies the body; finally
the holy war is—always from the point of view adopted here—
an external and collective manifestation of discernment between truth and error; it is like a centrifugal and negative
complement of the pilgrimage—complement, not contrary,
because it remains attached to the centre and is positive
through its religious content.

Let us recapitulate once again the essential characteristics of
Islam as seen from the angle which particularly concerns us
here. In normal conditions Islam strikes one by the unshakeable
character of its conviction and by the combative nature of its
faith; these two complementary aspects, the one inner and
static and the other outer and dynamic, are essentially derived
from a consciousness of the Absolute, which on the one hand
establishes inaccessibility to doubt and on the other repels

---

[1] The same applies on the plane of the human microcosm both to the
intelligence and to the will: neither desire nor discernment are exercised in the
absence of an object.

[2] Ramadan in the Moslem year is what Sunday is in the Christian week or
the Sabbath in the Jewish week.

error with violence;[1] the Absolute—or consciousness of the Absolute—thus engenders in the soul the qualities of rock and of lightning, the former being represented by the *kaaba*, which is the centre, and the latter by the sword of the holy war, which marks the periphery. On the spiritual plane Islam lays stress on knowledge, since it is knowledge which realizes the maximum of unity in the sense that it pierces the illusion of plurality and goes beyond the duality of subject and object; love is a form and a criterion of unitive knowledge or, from another point of view, a stage on the way to it. On the earthly plane Islam seeks equilibrium and puts each thing in its own place; moreover it makes a clear distinction between the individual and the community while also taking account of their reciprocal solidarity. *El-Islâm* is the human condition brought into equilibrium in function of the Absolute, both in man's soul and in society.

The basis of spiritual ascent is that God is pure Spirit and that man resembles Him fundamentally through the intelligence; man goes towards God by means of that which is, in him, most conformable to God—the intellect—which is at the same time both penetration and contemplation and has as its 'supernaturally natural' content the Absolute which illumines and delivers. The character of a way depends on a particular preliminary definition of man: if man is defined as passion, as the general perspective of Christianity would have it—though there is here no principial restriction—then the way is suffering; if as desire, then the way is renunciation; if as will, then the way is effort; if as intelligence, then the way is discernment, concentration, contemplation. This could also be expressed as follows: the way is such-and-such 'to the extent that'—not 'because'—man has such-and-such a nature; this enables us to understand why Moslem spirituality, though founded on the mystery of knowledge, none the less also includes both renunciation and love.

The Prophet said: 'God has created nothing more noble than intelligence, and His wrath is on him who despises it', and he also said: 'God is beautiful and He loves beauty.' These two sayings are characteristic for Islam: for it the world is a huge

[1] In this perspective error is the negating of the Absolute or the attribution of an absolute character to the relative or the contingent, or the admitting of more than one Absolute. This metaphysical intention must not, however, be confused with the associations of ideas to which it can give rise in the consciousness of Moslems, associations that can have a purely symbolic meaning.

book filled with 'signs' (*ayāt*), or symbols—elements of beauty—
which speak to our understanding and are addressed to 'them
that understand'. The world is made up of forms, and they are
as it were the debris of a celestial music that has become
frozen; knowledge or sanctity dissolves our frozen state and
liberates the inner melody.[1] Here we must recall the verse in
the Quran which speaks of the 'stones from which streams
spring forth', though there are hearts which are 'harder than
stones', a passage reminiscent of the 'living water' of Christ and
of the 'well of water springing up into everlasting life' in the
hearts of saints.[2]

These 'streams' or 'living waters' are beyond all formal and
separating crystallizations; they belong to that domain of
'essential truth' (*haqīqah*) towards which the 'way' (*tarīqah*)
leads—starting out from the 'general road' (*sharī'ah*) formed by
the general Law—and at this level truth is no more a system of
concepts (a system moreover intrinsically adequate and indispensable) but rather an 'element' like fire or water. And this
leads us to a further consideration: if there are different religions—each of them by definition speaking an absolute and so
an exclusive language—this is because the difference between
the religions exactly corresponds by analogy to the differences
between human individuals. In other words, if the religions are
true it is because each time it is God who has spoken, and, if
they are different it is because God has spoken in different
'languages' in conformity with the diversity of the receptacles.
Finally, if they are absolute and exclusive, it is because in each
of them God has said 'I'. We know all too well, and it is moreover in the natural order of things, that this thesis is not
acceptable on the level of exoteric orthodoxies,[3] but it is so on

[1] The dervish songs and dances are symbolical, and so spiritually efficacious,
anticipations of the rhythms of immortality, and also—what amounts to the
same thing—of the divine nectar which secretly flows in the arteries of all
created things. Herein, moreover, lies an example of a certain opposition between the esoteric and exoteric orders which cannot fail to arise incidentally:
both music and dance are proscribed by the common Law, but esotericism
makes use of them as it does of the symbolism of wine, which is a forbidden
drink. In this there is nothing absurd, for in one respect the world too is
opposed to God, though 'made in His image'. Exotericism follows the 'letter'
and esotericism the 'divine intention'.

[2] Jalāl ed-Dīn Rūmī said: 'The ocean that I am is drowned in its own waves.
Strange limitless ocean that I am!'

[3] This word indicates a limitation. but *a priori* contains no reproach, for
the human bases are what they are.

the level of universal orthodoxy, that to which Mohyiddīn ibn Arabī, the great enunciator of gnosis in Islam, bore witness in these terms: 'My heart is open to every form: it is a pasture for gazelles (i.e. spiritual states), and a cloister for Christian monks, a temple for idols, the *kaaba* of the pilgrim, the tables of the Torah, and the book of the Quran. I practise the religion of Love;[1] in whatsoever direction His caravans advance,[2] the religion of Love shall be my religion and my faith.'[3]

[1] Here it is not a question of *mahabbah* in the psychological or methodological sense but of truth that is lived and of divine 'attraction'. Here 'love' is opposed to 'forms' which are envisaged as 'cold' and as 'dead'. St Paul also says that 'the letter killeth, but the spirit maketh alive'. 'Spirit' and 'love' are here synonymous.

[2] Literally: 'His camels'. 'Camels', like the 'gazelles' above, here indicate realities of the spirit; they represent the inner and outer consequences—or the dynamic modes—of 'love' or in other words of 'essential consciousness'.

[3] In the same way Jalāl ed-Dīn Rūmī says in his quatrains: 'If the image of our Beloved is in the temple of idols, it is an absolute error to circumambulate the *Kaaba*. If the *Kaaba* is deprived of His perfume, it is a synagogue. And, if in the synagogue we feel the perfume of union with Him, the synagogue is our *Kaaba*.' In the Quran this universalism is especially formulated in these two verses: 'To God belongeth the East and the West; whithersoever ye turn, there is the Countenance of God' (11, 115)—'Say: Call "*Allāh*" or call "*Er-Rahmān*"; whatever the Name ye call, to Him belong the most beautiful Names' (XVII, 110). In this second verse the Divine Names can signify spiritual perspectives and so the religions. The various religions are like the beads of the rosary; the cord is gnosis, their single essence passing through them all.

Chapter 2

The Quran

~~THE great theophany of Islam is the Quran; it presents itself as being a 'discernment' (furqān) between truth and error.~~[1]
In a sense the whole of the Quran—one of the names of which is indeed *El-Furqān* (the Discernment)—is a sort of multiple paraphrase of the fundamental discernment expressed by the *Shahādah*; its whole content is summed up in the words: '~~Truth has come and error~~ (*el-bātil*, the empty, or the inconsistent) ~~has vanished away; verily, error is ephemeral.~~' (Quran, XXVII, 73.)[2]
Before the message of the Quran is considered, attention must be given to its form and to the principles determining that form. An Arab poet once claimed that he could write a book superior to the Quran, disputing its excellence even from the mere point of view of style. Such a judgment, which is clearly contrary to the traditional thesis of Islam, is explicable in the case of a man who does not know that the excellence of a sacred book is not *a priori* of a literary order; many indeed are the texts conveying a spiritual meaning in which logical clarity is joined to powerful language or grace of expression without their having on this account a sacred character. That is to say, ~~the sacred Scriptures are not such because of the subject of which they treat or the manner in which they treat it but by reason of their level of inspiration,~~ or what amounts to the same thing, by virtue of their divine provenance; it is this which determines the content of the book, not the converse; like the Bible the Quran may speak of very many things other than God; it speaks of the devil, of the holy war, of the laws of succession and so on with-

---

[1] In this context it is significant that in Islam God Himself is often called *El-Haqq*, The Truth. The Sufi El-Hallaj exclaimed: *Anā El-Haqq*, 'I am the Truth', not 'I am Love'.
[2] Or, in another passage: '. . . We (*Allāh*) strike error with Truth that it may be crushed, and lo! error vanisheth away' (XXI, 18).

out being on that account less sacred, whereas other works may treat of God and of sublime matters without being on that account the Divine Word.

For Moslem orthodoxy the Quran is not only the uncreated Word of God—uncreated though expressing itself through created elements such as words, sounds and letters—but also the model par excellence of the perfection of language. Seen from outside, however, this book appears (apart from approximately the last quarter, the form of which is highly poetic, though it is not poetry) to be a collection of sayings and stories that is more or less incoherent and at first approach in places incomprehensible; the reader who is not forewarned, whether he reads the text in translation or in Arabic, runs up against obscurities, repetitions, tautologies and, in most of the long *sūrats*, against a certain dryness without having at least the 'sensory consolation' of that beauty of sound which emerges from ritual and correctly intoned reading. But such difficulties are to be met in one degree or another in most sacred Scriptures.[1] The seeming incoherence of these texts[2]—for instance the Song of Songs or certain passages of the Pauline Epistles—always has the same cause, the incommensurable disproportion between the Spirit and the limited resources of human language: it is as though the poverty-stricken coagulation which is the language of mortal man were under the formidable pressure of the Heavenly Word broken into a thousand fragments, or as if God, in order to express a thousand truths, had but a dozen words at his command and so was compelled to make use of allusions

[1] There are two principal modes or levels of inspiration—one direct and the other indirect—represented in the case of the New Testament by the sayings of Christ and by the Apocalypse as regards the former mode and by the stories in the Gospels and by the Epistles as regards the latter. In Judaism this difference is expressed by comparing the inspiration of Moses to a luminous mirror and that of the other prophets to a darkened mirror. Among Hindu sacred books the texts of secondary inspiration (*smriti*) are in general more easily accessible and seem more homogeneous than the Veda, which is directly inspired (*shruti*), and this shows that the immediate intelligibility and readily perceived beauty of a text are in no way criteria of inspiration or of the level of inspiration.

[2] It is this 'incoherent' surface of the language of the Quran—not the grammar or the syntax—with which the poet mentioned above considered he should find fault. The style of the revealed Books is always normative. Goethe characterized very well the style of sacred texts in his *Westöstlicher Diwan*: 'Thy song turns like the vault of heaven; the origin and the end are ever identical.'

heavy with meaning, of ellipses, abridgements and symbolical syntheses. A sacred Scripture—and let us not forget that for Christianity Scripture includes not only the Gospels but the whole Bible with all its enigmas and seeming scandals—is a totality, a diversified image of Being, one diversified and transfigured for the sake of the human receptacle it is a light that wills to make itself visible to our clay, or wills to take the form of that clay; in other words it is a truth which, since it needs must address itself to beings compounded of clay, or of ignorance, has no means of expression other than the very substance of the natural error of which our soul is made.[1]

'God speaks tersely' say the Rabbis and this also explains both the bold ellipses (at first sight incomprehensible) and the superimposed levels of meaning found in the Revelations;[2] moreover—and herein lies a crucial principle—for God the truth is in the spiritual or social efficacy of the words or the symbol, not in the factual exactitude when this is psychologically inoperative or even harmful; God's first wish is to save, not to instruct, and His concern is with wisdom and immortality, not with external knowledge, still less with satisfying human curiosity. Christ called his body 'the Temple', which may seem astonishing when one thinks that this term primarily, and to all appearances with better reason, designated a stone building; but the stone Temple was much less than Christ, the receptacle of the living God—for Christ was come—and in reality the term 'Temple' applied with far more reason to Christ than to the building made by the hands of men; it can even be said that the Temple, whether that of Solomon or that of Herod, was the

[1] In his *Kitāb fīhi mā fīh* Jalāl ed-Dīn Rūmī wrote: 'The Quran is like a young married woman: even if you try to unveil her she will not show herself to you. If you discuss the Quran you will discover nothing and no joy will come to you. That is because you have tried to pull off the veil and the Quran refuses itself to you; by employing cunning and making itself ugly in your sight and undesirable it is saying to you: "I am not that which you love." And it can in this manner show itself under any kind of light.' See also *Discourses of Rūmī* (Murray, 1961) p. 236. According to the teaching of St Augustine and other Fathers, repeated by Pius XII in his Encyclical *Divino Afflante*: 'God has purposely strewn difficulties throughout the Holy Books He has Himself inspired in order that we may be stimulated to read and study them with greater attention and in order to exercise us in humility by the salutary recognition of the limited capacity of our intelligence.'

[2] For instance, it is said that the Bhagavadgītā can be read according to seven different threads of meaning. This principle has been mentioned several times in the author's previous works.

image of the body of Christ, temporal succession not entering into the matter for God; it is thus that sacred Scriptures at times displace words and even facts in function of a higher truth which eludes man. But it is not merely intrinsic difficulties that are found in the revealed Books, there is also the matter of their distance in time and the differences in mentality in different periods, or rather the qualitative inequality of different phases of the human cycle; at the origin of a tradition—whether we are speaking of the age of the Rishis or of that of Muhammad —the language was different from what it is today, the words were not well-worn and they then contained infinitely more than we can divine; many things which were clear for the reader of earlier times could be passed over in silence but need to be rendered explicit—not added to—at a later stage.[1]

A sacred text with its seeming contradictions and obscurities is in some ways like a mosaic, or even an anagram; but it is only necessary to consult the orthodox, and so divinely guided, commentaries in order to find out with what intention a particular affirmation was made and in what respects it is valid, or what are the underlying implications that enable one to connect elements which at first sight appear incongruous. These commentaries sprang from the oral tradition which from the beginning accompanied the Revelation, or else they sprang by inspiration from the same supernatural source; thus their role is not only to intercalate missing, though implicit, parts of the text and to specify in what relationship or in what sense a given thing should be understood, but also to explain the diverse symbolisms, often simultaneous and superimposed one on another: in short the commentaries providentially form part of the tradition; they are as it were the sap of its continuity, even if their committal to writing or in certain cases their remanifestation after some interruption occurred only at a relatively late date in order to meet the requirements of a particular historical period. 'The ink of the learned (in the Law or in the Spirit) is like the blood of the martyrs', said the Prophet, and

[1] We have no wish to devote space here to the deployment of unintelligence in modern textual criticism, whether it be 'psychological' or of some other kind. Suffice it to point out that in our times the devil has not only laid hold on charity, which he seeks to reduce to an atheistical and materialistic altruism, but has also swallowed up the exegesis of Holy Writ.

this indicates the capital part played in every traditional cosmos by orthodox commentaries.[1]

According to the Jewish tradition it is not the literal form of the holy Scriptures which has the force of law, but solely their orthodox commentaries. The Torah is a 'closed' book and does not open itself to a direct approach; it is the sages who 'open' it, for it is in the very nature of the Torah to require from the beginning the commentary of the Mischna. It is said that the Mischna was given out in the Tabernacle, when Joshua transmitted it to the Sanhedrin; by this the Sanhedrin was consecrated and thus instituted by God like the Torah and at the same time. And this is highly important: the oral commentary, which Moses had received on Sinai and transmitted to Joshua, was in part lost and had to be reconstituted by the sages on the basis of the Torah: this shows very clearly that gnosis includes both a 'horizontal' and a 'vertical' continuity, or rather that it accompanies the written Law in a manner that is both 'horizontal' and continuous and also 'vertical' and discontinuous; the secrets are passed from hand to hand, but the spark may at any time leap forth on mere contact with the revealed Text in function of a particular human receptacle and the imponderables of the Holy Spirit. It is also said that God gave the Torah during the day-time and the Mischna by night;[2] and again, that the Torah is infinite in itself whereas the Mischna is inexhaustible by its movement in time. We would add that the Torah is like the ocean, and the Mischna like a river. *Mutatis mutandis* all this applies to every Revelation and particularly to Islam. There must be authorities for the Faith (*imān*) and the Law (*islām*), but equally there must be authorities for the Way (*ihsān*), and these latter authorities are none other than the Sufis and their duly qualified representatives. The logical necessity for authorities in this third domain, which the theologians of 'the exterior' (*'ulamā ezh-zhāhir*) are forced to admit,

---

[1] Jalāl ed-Dīn Rūmī, in the work quoted above, wrote: 'God the Most High does not speak to just any man; like the kings of this world He does not speak with any casual fool; He has chosen ministers and deputies. Man accedes to God by going through the intermediaries He has appointed. God the Most High has made an election among his creatures in order that a man may come to Him by going through him whom He has chosen.' This passage, which refers to the Prophets, is also applicable to the authorized interpreters of the tradition.

[2] Here the reader will recall that Nicodemus came to find Christ by night, and this implies a reference to esotericism or to gnosis.

though they cannot explain it, is indeed one of the proofs of the legitimacy of Sufism, therefore also of its doctrines and methods as well as of its organizations and masters.

These considerations concerning the sacred Books call for some sort of definition of the epithet 'sacred' itself: that is sacred which in the first place is attached to the transcendent order, secondly, possesses the character of absolute certainty and, thirdly, eludes the comprehension and power of investigation of the ordinary human mind. Imagine a tree the leaves of which, having no kind of direct knowledge of the root, hold a discussion about whether or not a root exists and what is its form if it does: suppose a voice then came from the root telling them that the root does exist and what form it has; that message would be sacred. The sacred is the presence of the centre in the periphery, of the motionless in the moving; dignity is essentially an expression of it, for in dignity too the centre manifests at the exterior; the heart is revealed in gestures. The sacred introduces a quality of the absolute into relativities and confers on perishable things a texture of eternity.

In order to understand the full scope of the Quran we must take three things into consideration: its doctrinal content, which we find made explicit in the great canonical treatises of Islam such as those of Abu Hanīfah and Et-Tahāwī; its narrative content, which depicts all the vicissitudes of the soul; and its divine magic or its mysterious and in a sense miraculous power;[1] these sources of metaphysical and eschatological wisdom, of mystical psychology and theurgic power lie hidden under a veil of breathless utterances, often clashing in shock, of crystalline and fiery images, but also of passages majestic in rhythm, woven of every fibre of the human condition.

But the supernatural character of this Book does not lie only in its doctrinal content, its psychological and mystical truth and its transmuting magic, it appears equally in its most

---

[1] Only this power can explain the importance of the recitation of the Quran. In his *Risālat el-Quds* Ibn Arabī quotes the case of Sufis who spent their whole life in reading or in ceaselessly reciting the Quran, and this would be inconceivable and even impossible of realization were there not, behind the husk of the literal text, a concrete and active spiritual presence which goes beyond the words and the mind. Moreover it is by virtue of this power of the Quran that certain verses can chase away demons and heal the sick, given the concurrence of the requisite conditions.

exterior efficacy, in the miracle of the expansion of Islam; the effects of the Quran in space and time bear no relation to the mere literary impression which the written words themselves can give to a profane reader. Like every sacred Scripture the Quran is also *a priori* a 'closed' book, though 'open' in another respect, that of the elementary truths of salvation.

It is necessary to distinguish in the Quran between the general excellence of the Divine Word and the particular excellence of a content which may be superimposed, as, for instance, when it is a question of God or of his qualities; it is like the distinction between the excellence of gold and that of some masterpiece made from gold. The masterpiece directly manifests the nobility of gold; similarly the nobility of the content of one or another verse of the sacred book expresses the nobility of the Quranic substance, of the Divine Word, which is in itself undifferentiated; it cannot, however, add to the infinite value of that Word. This is also connected with the 'divine magic', the transforming and sometimes theurgic virtue of the divine speech to which allusion has already been made.

This magic is closely linked with the actual language of the Revelation, which is Arabic, and so translations are canonically illegitimate and ritually ineffectual. When God has spoken in it a language is sacred;[1] and in order that God should speak in it it must have certain characteristics such as are not found in any modern language; finally, it is essential to grasp that after a certain period in the cycle accompanied by a certain hardening in the situation on earth God has spoken no more, or at any rate not as Revealer; in other words, after a certain period whatever is put forward as new religion is inevitably false;[2]

---

[1] From this the reader might conclude that Aramaic is a sacred language since Christ spoke it, but here three reservations must be made; first, in Christianity, as in Buddhism, it is the Avatara himself who is the Revelation so that, apart from their doctrine, the Scriptures have not the central and plenary function which they have in other traditions; secondly, the precise Aramaic words used by Christ have not been preserved, which corroborates what has just been said; thirdly, for Christ himself Hebrew was the sacred language. Though the Talmud affirms that 'the Angels do not understand Aramaic', this language has none the less a particularly high liturgical value; long before Christ it was 'made sacred' by Daniel and Esdras.

[2] The same can be said of initiatic orders. One can—or rather God can—create a new branch of an ancient lineage or found a congregation of people around a pre-existing initiation, if there is an imperative reason for doing so and if this sort of congregation accords with the practice of the tradition in question, but in no circumstances has anyone a right to found a 'society' having

the Middle Ages mark *grosso modo* the final limit.[1] The Quran is, like the world, at the same time one and multiple. The world is a multiplicity which disperses and divides; the Quran is a multiplicity which draws together and leads to Unity. The multiplicity of the holy Book—the diversity of its words, sentences, pictures and stories—fills the soul and then absorbs it and imperceptibly transposes it into the climate of serenity and immutability by a sort of divine 'cunning'.[2] The soul, which is accustomed to the flux of phenomena, yields to this flux without resistance; it lives in phenomena and is by them divided and dispersed—even more than that, it actually becomes what it thinks and does. The revealed Discourse has the virtue that it accepts this tendency while at the same time reversing the movement thanks to the celestial nature of the content and the language, so that the fishes of the soul swim without distrust and with their habitual rhythm into the divine net.[3] To the degree that it can bear it the mind must have infused into it a consciousness of the metaphysical contrast between 'substance' and 'accidents'; a mind thus regenerated is a mind which keeps its thoughts first of all on God and thinks all things in Him. In other words, through the mosaic of texts, phrases and words, God extinguishes the agitation of the mind by Himself taking on the appearance of mental agitation. The Quran is like a picture of everything the human brain can think and feel, and it is by this means that God exhausts human disquiet, infusing into the believer silence, serenity and peace.

In Islam, as also in Judaism, Revelation relates essentially to the symbolism of the book; the whole universe is a book whose

'Self-Realization' as its aim, for the very simple reason that such a realization is exclusively the province of the traditional organizations; even if someone tried to incorporate a genuine initiation into the framework of a 'society' or of some kind of 'spiritual fellowship'—in fact a profane association—one can be certain that this very framework would wholly paralyse its efficacy and inevitably bring about deviations. Spiritual treasures do not accommodate themselves to just any sort of framework.

[1] In fact Islam is the last world religion. As for the Sikh brotherhood, this is an esotericism analogous to that of Kabīr, the special position of which is explained by the quite exceptional conditions arising from the contiguity of Hinduism and Sufism; but here too it is a case of the very latest possibility.

[2] In the sense of the Sanskrit term *upāya*.

[3] This is true of every sacred Scripture and is notably true of the Bible story: the vicissitudes of Israel are those of the soul seeking its Lord. In Christianity this function of 'transforming magic' appertains especially to the Psalms.

letters are the cosmic elements—the *dharmas* as Buddhists would say—which, by their innumerable combinations and under the influence of the divine Ideas, produce worlds, beings and things. The words and phrases of the book are the manifestations of the creative possibilities, the words in respect of the content, the phrases in respect of the container; the phrase is, in effect, like a space or a duration conveying a predestined series of compossibles and constituting what may be called a 'divine plan' This symbolism of the book is distinguished from that of speech by its static character; speech is situated in duration and implies repetition whereas books contain affirmations in a mode of simultaneity; in a book there is a certain levelling out, all the letters being alike, and this is moreover highly characteristic of the Islamic perspective. Only, this perspective, like that of the Torah, also includes the symbolism of speech; speech is however then identified with the origin; God speaks and His Speech is crystallized in the form of a Book. Clearly this crystallization has its prototype in God, and indeed it can be affirmed that the 'Speech' and the 'Book' are two sides of pure Being, which is the Principle that both creates and reveals; however, it is said that the Quran is the Word of God, not that the Word proceeds from the Quran or from the Book.

First of all the 'Word' is Being as the eternal Act of Beyond-Being, of the Divine Essence;[1] but, taken as the sum of the possibilities of manifestation, Being is the 'Book'. Then, on the level of Being itself, the Word, or according to another image the Pen,[2] is the creative Act while the Book is the creative Substance;[3] here there is a connection with *Natura naturans* and *Natura naturata* in the highest sense attributable to these concepts. Finally, on the level of Existence (or, it could be said, of Manifestation) the Word is the 'Divine Spirit', the central and universal Intellect which gives effect to and perpetuates the miracle of creation, as it were by 'delegation'; in this case the Book is the sum of the 'crystallized' possibilities, the world of innumerable creatures. The 'Word' is then the aspect of 'dynamic' simplicity or of simple 'action', while the 'Book' is the aspect of 'static' complexity or differentiated 'being'.

Or it can be said that God created the world like a Book and

---

[1] The *Gottheit* or *Urgrund* of Eckhart's doctrine.
[2] See also the chapter *En-Nûr* in the author's book *L'Oeil du Coeur*.
[3] According to Hindu doctrine this is the Divine *Prakriti*.

His Revelation came down into the world in the form of a Book; but man has to hear the Divine Word in Creation and by that Word ascend towards God; God became Book for man and man has to become Word for God; man is a 'book' through his microcosmic multiplicity and his state of existential coagulation whereas God, when envisaged in this context, is pure Word through His metacosmic Unity and His pure principial 'activity'.

In Christianity the place of the 'Book' is taken by the 'Body' with its two complements of 'flesh' and 'blood' or 'bread' and 'wine'; *in divinis* the Body is, first, the primary autodetermination of Divinity, and thus the first 'crystallization' of the Infinite; next it is Universal Substance, the true 'mystical Body of Christ; and finally it is the world of creatures, the 'crystallized' manifestation of this Body.

We have seen that God-as-Being is The Book *par excellence*, and that, on the level of Being, the pole of Substance is the first reflection of this Book; the Word, which is its dynamic complement, then becomes the Pen, the vertical axis of creation. In contra-distinction man too has an aspect of Word represented by his name; God created man in naming him; the soul is a Word of the Creator when envisaged from the aspect of its simplicity or its unity.

The most obvious content of the Quran is made up, not of doctrinal expositions, but of historical and symbolical narratives and eschatological imagery; the pure doctrine emerges from these two sorts of pictures in which it is enshrined. Setting aside the majesty of the Arabic text and its almost magical resonances a reader could well become wearied of the content did he not know that it concerns ourselves in a quite concrete and direct way, since the 'misbelievers' (the *kafirūn*), the 'associaters' of false divinities with God (the *mushrikūn*) and the hypocrites (the *munāfiqūn*) are within ourselves; likewise that the Prophets represent our intellect and our conscience, that all the tales in the Quran are enacted almost daily in our souls, that Mecca is our heart and that the tithe, the fast, the pilgrimage and the holy war are so many virtues, whether secret or open, or so many contemplative attitudes.

Running parallel with this microcosmic and alchemical interpretation there is the external interpretation which concerns the phenomena of the world around us. The Quran is the world, both outside and within us, always connected to God in the two respects of origin and end; but this world, or these two worlds, show fissures announcing death or destruction or, to be more precise, transformation, and this is what the apocalyptic and eschatological surats teach us; everything that concerns the world also concerns us, and conversely. These surats transmit to us a multiple and striking picture of the fragility both of our earthly condition and of matter, a picture too of the destined reabsorption of space and of the elements in the invisible substance of the causal 'protocosm'; this is the collapse of the visible world into the immaterial—a collapse, to paraphrase Saint Augustine, 'inwards' or 'upwards'; it is also the confronting of creatures, snatched from the earth, with the flashing reality of the Infinite.

By its 'surfaces' the Quran presents a cosmology which treats of phenomena and their final end, and, by its 'pinnacles', a metaphysic of the real and the unreal.

Not surprisingly the imagery of the Quran is inspired above all by conflict; Islam was born in an atmosphere of conflict and the soul in search of God must fight. Islam did not invent strife; the world is a constant disequilibrium, for to live means to struggle. But this struggle is only one aspect of the world and it vanishes with the level to which it belongs; the whole of the Quran is also suffused with a tone of 'powerful' serenity. In psychological terms it could be said that the combative aspect of the Moslem is counterbalanced by his fatalism; in the spiritual life the 'holy war' of the spirit against the seducing soul (*ennafs el-'ammārah*) is outpassed and transfigured by peace in God, by consciousness of the Absolute; it is as if in the last analysis it were no more we who were fighting, and this brings us back to the symbiosis of 'combat' and 'knowledge' in the Bhagavadgītā and also to certain aspects of the knightly arts in Zen. The practice of Islam at whatever level means to be at rest in effort; Islam is the way of equilibrium and of light resting on that equilibrium.

Equilibrium is the link between disequilibrium and union, just as union is the link between equilibrium and unity, which is the 'vertical' dimension. Disequilibrium and equilibrium, lack of rhythm and rhythm, separation and union, division and unity: such are the great themes of the Quran and of Islam. Everything in being and in becoming is envisaged in terms of Unity and its gradations or the mystery of its negation.

In the case of the Christian what is necessary for coming to God is 'unreservedly to renounce oneself', as St John of the Cross put it; and the Christian is astonished to hear from the Moslem that the key to salvation is to believe that God is One; what he cannot know straight away is that all depends on the quality—on the 'sincerity' (ikhlāṣ)—of this belief; what saves is the purity or the totality of the belief, and that totality clearly implies the loss of self, whatever the form in which this is expressed.

As for the negation of the Christian Trinity in the Quran—and this negation is extrinsic and conditional—we must take account of certain shades of meaning. The Trinity can be envisaged according to a 'vertical' perspective or according to either of two 'horizontal' perspectives, the former of them being supreme and the other not. The 'vertical' perspective—Beyond-Being, Being and Existence—envisages the hypostases as 'descending' from Unity or from the Absolute—or from the Essence it could be said—which means that it envisages the degrees of Reality; the supreme 'horizontal' perspective corresponds to the Vedantic triad Sat (supra-ontological Reality), Chit (Absolute Consciousness) and Ānanda (Infinite Bliss), which means that it envisages the Trinity inasmuch as It is hidden in Unity;[1] the non-supreme 'horizontal' perspective on the contrary places Unity as an essence hidden within the Trinity, which is then an ontological Trinity representing the three fundamental aspects or modes of Pure Being, whence we have the triad: Being, Wisdom, Will (Father, Son, Spirit). Now the concept of a Trinity seen as a 'deployment' (tajallī) of Unity or of the Absolute is in no way opposed to the unitary doctrine of Islam; what is opposed to it is solely the attribution of absoluteness to the Trinity alone, or even to the ontological Trinity alone, as it is envisaged exoterically. This last point of view does not, strictly speaking, reach to the Absolute and this is as much as to say that it attributes an absolute character to what is relative and ignores Māyā and the degrees of reality or

---

[1] The Absolute is not the Absolute inasmuch as it contains aspects, but inasmuch as It transcends them; inasmuch as It is Trinity It is therefore not Absolute.

of illusion; it does not conceive of the metaphysical (but not pantheistic),[1] identity between manifestation and the Principle, still less, therefore, does it conceive of the consequence this identity implies from the point of view of the intellect and the knowledge which delivers.

Here comment is called for on the subject of the 'misbelievers' the *kāfirūn*, those, that is, who, according to the Quran, do not belong, as do Jews and Christians, to the category of 'people of the Book' (*ahl el-Kitāb*). If the religion of these 'misbelievers' is false, or if misbelievers are such because their religion is false, why have Sufis declared that God can be present, not only in churches and synagogues, but also in the temples of idolaters? It is because in the 'classical' and 'traditional' cases of paganism the loss of the full truth and of efficacy for salvation essentially results from a profound modification in the mentality of the worshippers and not from an ultimate falsity of the symbols; in all the religions which surrounded each of the three Semitic forms of monotheism, as also in those forms of 'fetishism'[2] still alive today, a mentality once contemplative and so in possession of a sense of the metaphysical transparency of forms had ended by becoming passional, worldly[3] and, in the strict sense, superstitious.[4] The symbol through which the reality symbolized was originally clearly perceived—a reality of which it is more-over truly speaking an aspect—became in fact an opaque and uncomprehended image or an idol, and this falling away of the general level of mentality could not fail in its turn to react on the tradition itself, enfeebling it and falsifying it in various ways; most of the ancient paganisms were indeed characterized by intoxication with power and sensuality. There is, assuredly, a personal paganism to be met with even within those religions which are objectively living, just as, conversely, truth and piety

[1] Not pantheistic since it is in no sense 'material', nor even 'substantial' in the cosmological sense of that term.

[2] This word is here used only as a conventional sign to designate decadent traditions, and there is no intention of pronouncing on the value of any particular African or Melanesian tradition.

[3] According to the Quran the *kāfir* is in effect characterized by his 'worldli-ness', that is, by his preference for the good things of this world and his inadvertance (*ghaflah*) as regards those lying beyond this world.

[4] According to the Gospels the pagans imagine they will be answered 'for their much speaking'. At root 'superstition' consists in the illusion of taking the means for the end or of worshipping forms for their own sake and not for their transcendent content.

may be actualized in a religion which is objectively decadent, in which case however the integrity of its symbolism is to be presumed; but it would be wholly wrong to believe that any of the great world religions alive today could in its turn become pagan; they have not the time to become so, and their sufficient reason is in a sense that they should endure till the end of the world. That is why they are formally guaranteed by their founders, which is not the case with the great paganisms that have disappeared; these had no human founders and in their case their perennial subsistence was conditional, the primordial perspectives being 'spatial' and not 'temporal'; Hinduism alone of all the great traditions of the primordial type has had the possibility of renewing its vigour through the ages thanks to its avataras.[1] In any case it was not our intention here to enter into details but rather to make it clear why, from the point of view of some Sufi, it was not Apollo who was false but the way he was regarded.[2]

But to return to the 'people of the Book'. If the Quran contains elements of polemic concerning Christianity and, for stronger reasons, concerning Judaism, it is because Islam came after these religions, and this means that it was obliged—and there is a point of view which allows of its doing so—to put itself forward as an improvement on what came before it. In other words the Quran enunciates a perspective which makes it possible to 'go beyond' certain formal aspects of the two more ancient monotheisms. Something analogous can be seen, not only in the position of Christianity in relation to Judaism—where the point is self-evident by reason of the messianic idea and the fact that the former is like a 'bhaktic' esotericism of the latter—but also in the attitude of Buddhism towards Brahmanism; here too the later appearance in time coincides with a perspective that is symbolically, though not intrinsically,

[1] Moreover there is nothing to exclude the possibility of other branches of the primordial tradition, of 'Hyperborean' or 'Atlantean' affiliation, from having survived on the fringes of the historical scene, though this could not be so in the case of the great traditions of urbanized peoples. Apart from this, when paganism is mentioned—and we have adopted this conventional term without regard either to its etymology or its unpleasant associations, which chiefly arise from abuses—there is no doubt always need to make a reservation as regards a sapiential esotericism inaccessible to the majority and in fact incapable of acting on that majority.

[2] And also how he was represented, as is proved by 'classical' art.

superior. Of this fact the tradition that is apparently being superseded clearly has no need to take account since each perspective is a universe for itself—and thus a centre and a standard—and since in its own way it contains all valid points of view. By the very logic of things the later tradition is 'condemned' to the symbolical attitude of superiority,[1] on pain of non-existence one might almost say; but there is also a positive symbolism of anteriority and in this respect the new tradition, which is from its own point of view the final one, must incarnate 'what came before', or 'what has always existed'; its novelty—or glory—is consequently its absolute 'anteriority'.

Pure intellect is the 'immanent Quran'; the uncreated Quran —the Logos—is the Divine Intellect; and this is crystallized in the form of the earthly Quran and answers 'objectively' to that other immanent and 'subjective' revelation which is the human intellect.[2] In Christian terms it could be said that Christ is like the 'objectivation' of the intellect and the intellect is like the 'subjective' and permanent revelation of Christ. Thus there are two poles for the manifestation of Divine Wisdom and they are: first, the Revelation 'above us' and, secondly, the intellect 'within us'; the Revelation provides the symbols while the intellect deciphers them and 'recollects' their content, thereby again becoming conscious of its own substance. Revelation is a deployment and intellect a concentration; the descent is in accord with the ascent.

But there is another *haqīqah* (truth) on which we should wish to touch at this point, and it is this: in the sensory order the Divine Presence has two symbols or vehicles—or two 'natural manifestations'—of primary importance: the heart within us, which is our centre, and the air around us, which we breathe. The air is a manifestation of ether, the weaver of forms, and it is at the same time the vehicle of light, which also makes manifest

---

[1] This attitude is necessarily legitimate from a certain angle and at a certain level and is explained, in the field of monotheism, by the fact that the Jewish, Christian and Islamic religions correspond respectively to the ways of 'action', 'love' and 'knowledge' to the extent that they can, as exotericisms, do so and without prejudice to their most profound content.

[2] It is 'subjective' because empirically it is within us. The term 'subjective', as applied to the intellect, is as improper as the epithet 'human'; in both cases the terms are used simply in order to define the way of approach.

ether – the upper regions of space

the element ether.[1] When we breathe, the air penetrates us and, symbolically, it is as though it introduced into us the creative ether and the light too; we inhale the Universal Presence of God. Equally there is a connection between light and coolness, for the sensation of both is liberating; what is light externally is coolness inwardly. We inhale luminous, cool air and our respiration is a prayer, as is the beating of our heart; the luminosity relates to the Intellect and the freshness to pure Being. In Islam it is taught that at the end of time light will become separated from heat and heat will be hell whereas light will be Paradise; the light of heaven is cool and the heat of hell dark.

The world is a fabric woven of threads of ether, and into it we and all other creatures are woven. All sensory things come forth from ether, which contains all; everything is ether crystallized. The world is an immense carpet; we possess the whole world in each breath because we breathe the ether from which all things are made,[2] and we 'are' ether. Just as the world is an immeasurable carpet in which everything is repeated in a rhythm of continual change, or where everything remains similar within the framework of the law of differentiation, so too the Quran—and with it the whole of Islam—is a carpet or fabric, in which the centre is everywhere repeated in an infinitely varied way and in which the diversity is no more than a development of the unity. The universal 'ether', of which the physical element is only a distant and grosser reflection, is none other than the divine Word which is everywhere 'being' and 'consciousness' and everywhere 'creative' and 'liberating' or 'revealing' and 'illuminating'.

The nature which surrounds us—sun, moon, stars, day and night, the seasons, the waters, mountains, forests and flowers— is a kind of primordial Revelation; now these three things— nature, light and breath—are profoundly linked with one another. Breathing should be linked with the remembrance of God; we should breathe with reverence, with the heart so to speak. It is said that the Spirit of God—the Divine Breath— was 'over the waters' and that it was by breathing into it that

---

[1] The Greeks passed over the element ether in silence, no doubt because they conceived it as being hidden in the air, which is also invisible. In Hebrew the word *avir* designates both air and ether: the word *aor* has the same root and means 'light'.

[2] This is a symbolic manner of speech, for ether being perfect plenitude is motionless and could not move.

God created the soul, as it is also said that man, who is 'born of the Spirit', is like the wind; 'thou hearest the sound thereof, but canst not tell whence it cometh, and whither it goeth'.

It is significant that Islam is defined in the Quran as an 'enlarging (*inshirāh*) of the breast', that it is said, for example, that God 'hath enlarged our breast for Islam'; the connection between the Islamic perspective and the initiatic meaning of breathing and also of the heart is a key of the first importance for understanding the arcana of Sufism. It is true that by the very force of things the same path also opens out on to universal gnosis.

The 'remembrance of God' is like breathing deeply in the solitude of high mountains: here the morning air, filled with the purity of the eternal snows, dilates the breast; it becomes space and heaven enters our heart.

This picture includes yet another symbolism, that of the 'universal breath': here expiration relates to cosmic manifestation or the creative phase and inspiration to reintegration, to the phase of salvation or the return to God.

One reason why Western people have difficulty in appreciating the Quran and have even many times questioned whether this book does contain the premises of a spiritual life[1] lies in the fact that they look in a text for a meaning that is fully expressed and immediately intelligible, whereas Semites, and Eastern peoples in general, are lovers of verbal symbolism and read 'in depth'. The revealed phrase is for them an array of symbols from which more and more flashes of light shoot forth the further the reader penetrates into the spiritual geometry of the words: the words are reference points for a doctrine that is inexhaustible; the implicit meaning is everything, and the obscurities of the literal meaning are so many veils marking the majesty of the content.[2] But, even without taking into consideration the sibylline structure of very many sacred sentences, we can say that the Oriental extracts much from a few words:

[1] Louis Massignon answers this question in the affirmative.

[2] Thus, moreover, was the Bible read—following in the footsteps of antiquity —in the Middle Ages. The denial of the hermeneutical interpretation, which was the bulwark of traditional and integral intellectuality, inevitably led in the end to 'criticism'—and destruction—of the sacred Texts; for instance there is nothing left of the Song of Songs once only the literal meaning is accepted.

when, for example, the Quran recalls that 'the world beyond is better for you than this lower world' or that 'earthly life is but a play' or affirms: 'In your wives and your children ye have an enemy' or: 'say: Allah! then leave them to their empty play', or, finally, when it promises Paradise to 'him who has feared the station of his Lord and refused desire to his soul'—when the Quran speaks thus, there emerges for the Moslem[1] a whole ascetic and mystical doctrine, as penetrating and as complete as no matter what other form of spirituality worthy the name.

Man alone has the gift of speech, for he alone among all the creatures of this earth is 'made in the image of God' in a direct and total manner; and, since it is by virtue of this likeness (provided it is actualized by appropriate means) that man is saved—by virtue, that is, of the objective intelligence, associated with freewill and truthful speech, whether articulated or not—it is easy to understand the capital part played in the life of the Moslem by those sublime words—the verses of the Quran; they are not merely sentences which transmit thoughts, but are in a way, beings, powers or talismans; the soul of the Moslem is, as it were, woven of sacred formulae; in these he works, in these he rests, in these he lives and in these he dies.

It was the objectivity of human intelligence which enabled Adam to 'name' all things and all creatures; in other words it is this which enables man to know objects, plants and animals, though they do not know him; but the highest content of this intelligence is the Absolute; to be able to compass the greater is to be able to compass the lesser, and it is because man can know God that he knows the world. After its own fashion human intelligence is a proof of God.

At the beginning of this book we saw that the intention of the formula *Lā ilaha illā 'Llāh* becomes clear if by the term *ilah*—the literal meaning of which is 'divinity'—one understands reality, the level or nature of which remains to be determined. The first proposition of the sentence, which is negative in form ('There is no divinity . . .'), relates to the world and reduces it to nothingness by taking away from it any positive character; the second proposition, which is affirmative ('. . . save The Divinity, *Allāh*'), is related to Absolute Reality or to Being. The word 'divinity' (*ilah*) can be replaced by any word expressing a positive idea; in the first part of the formula this word

[1] Note that we say 'for the Moslem', not 'for every Moslem'.

would then remain indefinite, but in the second proposition it would become defined absolutely and exclusively as Principle,[1] as in the case of the Name *Allāh* (The Divinity) in respect of the word *ilah* (divinity). In the *Shahādah* there is metaphysical discernment between the unreal and the Real, and there is also combative virtue; this formula is both the sword of knowledge and the sword of the soul, whilst it marks too the peace that Truth brings, serenity in God. We have already seen that the first 'Testimony' is directly followed by the second—that of the Prophet—which it includes implicitly and which issues from it as if by polarization.

Another fundamental proposition of Islam—and no doubt the most important after the double Testimony of the faith—is the formula of consecration the *Basmalah*: 'In the Name of God, the infinitely Good,[2] the ever Merciful' (*Bismi 'Llāhi 'Rrahmāni 'Rrahīm*).[3] This is the formula of the Revelation, found at the head of every surat of the Quran except one which is considered as a continuation of its predecessor; this consecration is the first phrase of the revealed Book, for with it begins 'That which opens' (*Sūrat el-Fātihah*), the introductory surat. It is said that the *Fātihah* contains in essence the whole of the Quran, that the *Basmalah* in turn contains the whole of the *Fātihah*, that the Basmalah is itself contained in the first letter *bā* and that this is contained in its diacritical point.[4]

The *Basmalah* forms a kind of complement to the *Shahādah*: the *Shahādah* is an intellectual 'ascent' and the *Basmalah* an ontological 'descent'; in Hindu terms the former could be called *Shaiva* and the latter *Vaishnava*. If we may be permitted to

[1] One of the works of the Shaikh El-Allaoui contains indeed a whole litany drawn from the *Shahādah*: *Lā quddūsa* (holy) *illā 'Llāh*; *lā 'alīma* (wise) *illā 'Llāh*, and so on through all the divine attributes.

[2] Here we give the metaphysical meaning of this Name. No objection can be raised to the translating of the Name *Rahmān* as 'Compassionate' for compassion is as it were the essence of mercy.

[3] From this is derived the word *basmalah*, which means the act of saying: *Bismi 'Llāhi*. . . . The Arabic spelling is: *Bismi Allāhi al-Rahmāni al-Rahīm*.

[4] The letter *bā*, the second letter in the Arabic alphabet (the first being the *ālif*, a plain vertical line with an axial symbolism) is formed by a horizontal line slightly curved like a bowl and is distinguished by a point beneath it. Alī, the Prophet's son-in-law, and at a later date the Sufi Esh-Shīblī both compared themselves to this point under the *bā* in order to express their state of 'supreme Identity'. This diacritical point corresponds to the first drop of the divine Ink (*Midād*) to fall from the Pen; it is the Divine Spirit (*Er- Rūh*), or the Prototype of the world.

return once again to two Vedantic formulas of the highest importance, let us add that the *Shahādah* destroys the world because 'the world is false, Brahma is true', whereas the *Basmalah* on the contrary consecrates and sanctifies the world because 'all is *Ātmā*'; but the *Basmalah* is already contained in the *Shahādah* in the word *illā* (a contracted form of *in lā*, 'if not') which is the 'isthmus' *(barzakh)* between the negative and positive propositions of the formula, the first half of this word itself being positive *(in*, 'if') and the second negative *(lā*, 'no' or 'none'). In other words the *Shahādah* is the juxtaposition of the negation *lā ilaha* (no divinity) and the Name *Allāh* (The Divinity), this confrontation being linked by a word the first half of which, being positive, indirectly relates to *Allāh* and the second half, being negative, indirectly relates to 'unreality'; thus in the centre of the *Shahādah* there is a kind of inverted image of the relationship which it expresses, and this inversion represents the truth according to which the world possesses the degree of reality proper to its own level, since nothing can be cut off from the Divine Cause.

And it is from this mysterious heart of the *Shahādah* that the second *Shahādah* springs, like Eve drawn from the side of Adam. The Divine Truth, having said 'no' to the world which would be God, says 'yes' within the very framework of this 'no' because the world cannot in itself be cut off from God; *Allāh* cannot not be there in a certain fashion or in conformity with certain principles resulting both from His nature and from that of the world.

From a somewhat different point of view it can also be said that the *Basmalah* is the divine and revealing ray which bears into the world the truth of the double *Shahādah*:[1] the *Basmalah* is the 'descending' ray and the *Shahādah* is its content, the horizontal image which, in the world, reflects the Truth of God; in the second *Shahādah* (*Muhammadun Rasūlu 'Llāh*) this vertical ray is itself reflected and the projection of the Message becomes a part of the Message. The *Basmalah* consecrates everything including especially the vital functions with their inevitable and legitimate pleasures. Through this consecration

[1] In the same way that Christ is the Word borne into the world by the Holy Spirit. In this case the *Shahādah* is the Message made manifest; on the other hand, when it was said above that the *Basmalah* is contained in the first *Shahādah*—like the second *Shahādah* in the word *illā*—this referred to the *Shahādah in divinis*, envisaged, that is to say, as the Unmanifest Truth.

something of the divine Bliss enters into their enjoyment (it is as though God entered into the enjoyment and participated in it, or as though man entered a little, but of full right, into the Bliss of God.) Like the *Basmalah* the second *Shahādah* 'neutralizes' the denial enunciated by the first *Shahādah*, which symbolically speaking already bears within itself its 'compensatory dimension' or its 'corrective' in the word *illā* from which springs forth the *Muhammadun rasūlu 'Llāh*.

This question could also be approached from a rather different angle: the consecration 'In the Name of God, the infinitely Merciful, the ever Merciful in action' presupposes something in relation to which the idea of Unity, enunciated by the *Shahādah*, has to be realized, and this relationship is indicated in the *Basmalah* itself in the sense that, being divine utterance, it creates that which should then be brought back to the Uncreated. The divine Names *Rahmān* and *Rahīm*, both derived from the word *Rahmah* ('Mercy'), mean, the former the intrinsic Mercy of God and the latter His extrinsic Mercy; thus the former indicates an infinite quality and the latter a limitless manifestation of that quality. The words could also be respectively translated as 'Creator through Love' and 'Saviour through Mercy', or, drawing inspiration from a *hadīth*, we could comment on them thus: *Er-Rahmān* is the Creator of the world inasmuch as *a priori* and once for all He has furnished the elements of well-being of this lower world, while *Er-Rahīm* is the Saviour of men inasmuch as He confers on them the bliss of the world beyond, or gives them here below the seeds of that other world or dispenses its benefits.

In the Names *Rahmān* and *Rahīm* the divine Mercy confronts human incapacity in the sense that consciousness of our incapacity is, when coupled with confidence, the moral receptacle of Mercy. The Name *Rahmān* is like a sky full of light; the Name *Rahīm* is like a warm ray coming from the sky and giving life to man.

In the Name *Allāh* there are the aspects of awful Transcendence and enveloping Totality; were there only the aspect of Transcendence it would be difficult, if not impossible, to contemplate this Name. From a different point of view it can be said that the Name *Allāh* breathes forth at one and the same time serenity, majesty and mystery: the first of these qualities relates to the undifferentiation of substance, the second to the loftiness of the Principle and the third to the Ipseity, which is both secret and dazzling. In the written form of the Name *Allāh* in Arabic we distinguish a horizontal line, that of the very motion of writing, then the upright strokes of the *ālif* and the *lam*, and then finally a more or less circular line, symbolically reducible to a circle; these three elements are like indications of three 'dimensions': serenity, which is 'horizontal' and un-differentiated like the desert or a blanket of snow;[1] majesty, which is 'vertical' and motionless like a mountain:[2] and mystery, which extends 'in depth' and relates to the Divine Ipseity and to gnosis. The mystery of Ipseity implies that of identity, for the divine nature, which is totality as well as transcendence, includes all possible divine aspects including the world with its numberless individualized refractions of the Self.

The *Fātihah*, 'That which opens' (the Quran), has, as has already been pointed out, a capital importance, for it constitutes the unanimous prayer of Islam. It is composed of seven propositions or verses: 1. 'Praise to God, Master of the worlds; 2. The Infinitely Good, The ever Merciful; 3. The King of the Last Judgment; 4. It is Thee Whom we adore, and it is in Thee that we seek refuge; 5. Lead us on the straight way; 6. The way of those on whom is Thy Grace; 7. Not of those on whom is Thy Wrath, nor of those who stray.'

'Praise to God, Master of the worlds': the starting point of this formula is our state of existential enjoyment; to exist is to enjoy, for breathing, eating, living, seeing beauty, carrying out some work—all this is enjoyment; now what it is important to know is that every perfection or satisfaction, every quality, whether within us or outside, is only the effect of a trans-cendent and unique cause, and that this cause, the only cause there is, produces and determines numberless worlds of perfection.

'The Infinitely Good, the ever Merciful': The Good signifies that in advance God has given us existence and all the qualities and conditions this implies, and, since we exist and are also endowed with intelligence, we ought not to forget these gifts

---

[1] This is what is expressed by the verse already quoted: 'Say: *Allāh*! Then leave them to their vain talk' (VI, 91), or by this other verse: 'Is it not in the remembrance of *Allāh* that hearts rest in security?' (XIII, 28).

[2] '*Allāh*! There is no divinity save He, The Living (*El-Hayy*), The Self-Subsistent (*El-Qayyūm*).' (Quran, 11, 255 and 111, 1).

nor attribute them to ourselves; we did not create ourselves, nor did we invent either the eye or light. 'The Merciful': God gives us our daily bread, and not that alone: He gives us our eternal life, our participation in Unity and so in what is our true nature.

'The King of the Last Judgment': God is not only the Master of the worlds, He is also the Master of their end; He deploys them, then He destroys them. We, who are in existence, cannot not know that all existence runs to its end, that both microcosms and macrocosms terminate in a sort of divine nothingness. To know that the relative comes from the Absolute and depends on It is to know that the relative is not the Absolute and disappears in face of It.[1]

'It is Thee we adore and it is in Thee we seek refuge': adoration is the recognition of God outside us and above us, and thus submission to the infinitely distant God, whereas refuge is the return to the God within us, at the deepest level of our heart; it is confidence in a God Who is infinitely near. The 'external' God is like the infinity of the sky; the 'inward' God is like the intimacy of the heart.

'Lead us on the straight way': this is the way of ascent, the way which leads to liberating Unity; it is the union of will, love and knowledge.

'The way of those on whom is Thy Grace': the straight way is that where Grace draws us upwards; it is through Grace alone that we can follow this way; but we must open ourselves to that Grace and conform to its requirements.

'Not of those on whom is Thy Wrath, nor of those who stray': not of those who oppose Grace and by that fact place themselves in the ray of Justice or of Rigour, or who sever the bond linking them to pre-existing Grace through wanting to be independent of their Cause, or wanting to be themselves the cause; they fall like stones, deaf and blind; the Cause abandons them. 'Nor of those who stray': these are they who, without directly opposing the One, are none the less, through feebleness, lost in multiplicity; these do not deny the One, nor do they want to usurp Its rank, but they remain what they are, following their multiple nature as though not endowed with intelligence; briefly, they live beneath themselves and give themselves up

[1] The reader will have noticed that 'the Last Judgment' includes a temporal symbolism as against the spatial symbolism of 'Master of the Worlds'.

to cosmic powers, though without being lost if they submit to God.[1]

Formulas run through the life of the Moslem like weft through warp. As has been pointed out the *Basmalah* inaugurates and sanctifies every enterprise, it ritualizes the regular actions of life such as the ablutions and meals the formula (*el-hamdu lil Lah*) 'Praise to God' brings them to a close in relating their positive quality to the Sole Cause of all quality and thus 'sublimating' all enjoyment so that everything can be undertaken according to grace, the effect on earth of the Divine Bliss; in this sense all things are done as symbols of that Bliss.[2] These two formulas mark the two phases of consecration and deconsecration, the *coagula* and the *solve*; the *Basmalah* evokes the Divine Cause—and therefore the presence of God—in transitory things and the *Hamd*—the praise—in a sense dissolves these things by reducing them to their Cause.

The formulas *Subhāna 'Llāh* (Glory to God) and *Allāhu akbar* (God is greater) are often associated with the *Hamd*, in conformity with a *hadīth*, and recited with it. 'Glory to God' is said to nullify a heresy that is contrary to the Divine Majesty; thus this formula more especially concerns God in Himself; it separates Him from created things whereas the *Hamd* on the contrary connects them to God in a certain fashion. The formula 'God is greater'—the *Takbīr*—'opens' the canonical prayer and marks the change during prayer from one ritual position to another; it expresses by the comparative of the word 'great' (*kabīr*)—often taken, moreover, in the sense of a superlative—that God will always be 'greater', or 'the greatest', (*akbar*), and so shows itself to be a kind of paraphrase of the *Shahādah*.

---

[1] According to the Islamic interpretation these three categories of Grace, Wrath and Straying concern respectively the Moslems, who follow the middle way, the Jews, who rejected Jesus, and the Christians, who made a God of him; the choice of the symbols is admissible from an exoteric point of view, but the meaning is universal and refers to the three fundamental tendencies in man.

[2] Cf. the Bhagavadgītā (IX, 27, 28): 'Whatever thy work, thine eating, thy sacrifice, thy gift, thine austerities, make of it an offering to Me, O son of Kunti. Thus thou shalt be released from the bonds of action, whether their fruit be good or bad; with a soul firmly set on renunciation thou shalt be delivered and attain to Me.' According to an idea current among Moslems a meal taken without the *Basmalah* is eaten in the company of Satan, and the same applies to any important action.

According to tradition all these formulas, when recited a certain number of times, miraculously wipe out sins, even if as numberless as the drops of water in the sea. Here there is an analogy with the indulgences attached in Catholicism to certain formulas or prayers.

Another formula of almost organic importance in the life of a Moslem is the following: *in shā'a 'Llāh* (if God wills it); in saying this the Moslem recognizes his dependence, his frailty and his ignorance in the face of God and at the same time abdicates all passional pretention: this is essentially the formula of serenity. It is also an affirmation that the end of all things is God, that it is He alone who is the absolutely certain limit of our existence; there is no future outside of Him.

If the formula 'If God wills it' concerns the future in so far as we project into it the present—represented by our desire which we actively affirm—the formula *kāna maktūb* (it was written) concerns the present in so far as in it we meet the future—represented by the destiny we passively undergo. Similarly the formula *mā shā'a 'Llāh* (What God has willed—'has come' being implied) places the idea of 'If God wills it' in the past and the present; the event, or its beginning, is past, but its unfolding, or our ascertaining of the past or continuing event, is in the present. Moslem 'fatalism', the soundness of which is corroborated by the fact that it is perfectly consistent with activity—history is there to prove it—is the logical consequence of the fundamental conception of Islam according to which everything depends on God and returns to Him.

Moslems, and especially those who observe the *sunna* even in its minutest ramifications,[1] live in a web of symbols, participating in the weaving, since they live them, and thus have the benefit of so many means of remembering God and the world beyond, even if only indirectly. To the Christian, living as he does morally in the empty space of vocational possibilities and so of the unforeseeable, this situation of the Moslem appears to be a superficial formalism or even pharisaical, but such an

[1] This El-Ghazzālī in particular extolled. The opposite opinion also exists that the legal minimum is enough for going to Paradise provided there is either great purity of soul, or great virtue, or profound inner knowledge. In this context let us recall that Moslems divide actions into five categories: 1. what is indispensable (*fardh* or *wājib*); 2. what is recommended (*sunnah, mustahabb*); 3. what is indifferent (*mubāh*); 4. what is inadvisable (*makrūh*); 5. what is forbidden (*harām*).

impression fails to take account of the fact that for Islam the will does not make 'improvisations';[1] it is determined or canalized with a view to contemplative peace of the spirit;[2] the external has only a schematic significance and the whole spiritual rhythm unfolds inwardly. To pronounce on every occasion certain formulas may amount to nothing, and will seem a mere nothing to one who conceives only of moral heroism, but from another point of view—that of virtual union with God through the constant 'remembrance' of things divine—this verbal way of introducing into life spiritual 'points of reference' is on the contrary a means of purification and of grace as to which no doubt can be entertained. That which is spiritually possible is by the same token legitimate and even, in the appropriate context, necessary.

One of the salient doctrines in the Quran is that of the Divine Omnipotence; this doctrine of the utter dependence of all things on God is enunciated in the Quran with a strictness that is exceptional in the 'climate' of monotheism. At the beginning of this book the problem of predestination was touched on in showing that, if man is subject to fate, it is because—or in so far as—he is not God, not inasmuch as he participates ontologically in the Divine Liberty; it was pointed out that to deny predestination would amount to pretending that God does not know 'future' events 'beforehand' and is therefore not omniscient; this would be an absurd conclusion, for time is merely one mode of extension of existence and the empirical succession of its contents is only illusory.

This question of predestination also raises that of the Divine Omnipotence: if God is all-powerful, why can he not abolish the ills from which creatures suffer? If it is inadmissible to suppose that he wants to do so but cannot, it is equally inconceivable that he could do so but does not want to, at any rate in so far as we place reliance on our human sensibility. The answer must be as follows: Omnipotence, being something definite,

---

[1] On this point, as on others, there is nothing absolute about the divergence in perspective, but the differences of accent are none the less real and profound.

[2] This is why the required attitude is called an *islām*, an abandonment to a pre-existing frame for the will; the root of this word is the same as that of the word *salām*, 'peace', and this indicates the idea of a 'supernatural release', an idea also contained in the word *inshirāh*, meaning the enlarging of the breast by the Islamic faith.

cannot be identified with the Absolute in the strictly metaphysical sense of that term; it is one quality among others,
which is as much as to say that, like Being to which it appertains, it belongs to the domain of relativity, though not on that
account falling outside the principial domain; in short it relates
to the personal God, the ontological Principle, which creates
and is personified in relation to creatures, not to the supra-
personal Divinity, which is the Absolute and Ineffable Essence.
Omnipotence, like every attribute relating to an attitude or an
activity, has its sufficient reason in the world and is exercised
in the world; it is dependent on Being and could not be exercised
beyond that. God, 'in creating' and 'having created' is all-
powerful in relation to what His work includes, but not so in
relation to that which, in the divine nature itself, provokes both
creation and the inner laws of creation; He does not govern that
which makes the metaphysical necessity of the world and of
evil; He governs neither relativity, of which He is, as ontological Principle, the first affirmation, nor the principial consequences of relativity; He can abolish this evil or that, but not evil
as such; but that is what He would abolish were He to abolish
all ills. To speak of 'the world' is to speak of 'relativity', of the
deployment of relativities, of differentiation and of the presence
of evil; since the world is not God it must include imperfection,
otherwise it would be reduced to God and thus cease to exist
(ex-sistere).

The great contradiction in man is that he wants the multiple
but does not want to pay the price of this in anguish; he wants
relativity with its savour of absoluteness or infinity, but not the
suffering arising from its sharp edges; he desires extension but
not limitation, as if the former could exist apart from the latter
and as if pure extension could be found on the plane of measur-
able things. The whole of modern civilization is built on this error,
which has become for it an article of faith and a programme.

Perhaps all this could be more precisely expressed if the
problem is formulated as follows: The Divine Essence—the
Beyond-Being—includes in Its indistinction and as a potentiality comprised within Its very infinity a principle of relativity; Being, which generates the world, is the first of the
relativities, that from which all the others flow; the function of
Being is to deploy in the direction of 'nothingness', or in an
'illusory' mode, the infinity of Beyond-Being, which thus

becomes transmuted into ontological and existential[1] possibilities. Since Being is the first relativity it cannot abolish relativity; as we have already seen, if it could do so it would abolish Itself and *a fortiori* bring creation to naught; what we call 'evil' is only the extreme term of limitation, and so of relativity; the Omnipotent can no more abolish relativity than He can prevent two and two from making four, for relativity, like truth, proceeds from His nature, and this amounts to saying that God has not the power not to be God. Relativity is the 'shadow' or 'contour' which allows the Absolute to affirm Itself as such, first before Itself and then in 'innumerable' gushings forth of differentiations.[2]

The whole of this doctrine can be found expressed in the Quranic formula: 'And He has power over all things' (*wa-Hua 'alā kulli shay' in qadīr*); in Sufic terms it is said that God, inasmuch as He is Powerful, and so Creator, is envisaged on the level of the 'attributes' (*ṣifāt*) and quite clearly these could not govern the Essence or Quiddity (*Dhāt*); the 'Power' (*qadr*) relates to 'all things', to the existential totality. If we say that the Omnipotent has not the power not to be all-powerful, creator, merciful and just and that He also cannot prevent Himself from creating and deploying His attributes in creation, it will no doubt be objected that God created the world 'in full freedom' and that in it He manifests Himself freely; but this is to confuse the principial determination of the divine perfection with freedom as regards facts or contents; the perfection of necessity, a reflection of the Absolute, is confused with the imperfection of constraint, a consequence of relativity. That God creates in perfect freedom means that He cannot be subject to any constraint, since nothing is situated outside Him and things appearing to be outside Him cannot attain to Him, the levels of reality being incommensurably unequal. The metaphysical cause of creation or of manifestation is in God, and therefore it does not prevent Him from being Himself, that is, from being free; it cannot be denied that this cause is comprised in the divine nature unless freedom is confused with caprice, as it too often is by theologians—at any rate *de facto* and by

[1] The former concern Being Itself—and these are the divine attributes such as Omnipotence and Mercy—and the latter concern Existence, the world, things.

[2] This expression is purely symbolical, for on the plane of the macrocosm as a whole we are already beyond the realm of earthly number.

implication—without recognizing the logical consequences of their sentimental and antimetaphysical anthropomorphism. Like 'Omnipotence' the 'Freedom' of God has no meaning except in relation to the relative; it must be insisted that none of these terms applies to the ultimate Aseity; this means, not that the intrinsic perfections crystallized in these attributes are absent beyond relativity—*quod absit*—but on the contrary that they only have their infinite plenitude in the Absolute and the Ineffable.[1]

The question of divine punishment is often associated with that of Omnipotence and also with that of Divine Wisdom and Goodness, and arguments such as the following are brought forward: what interest can an infinitely wise and good God have in keeping a record of our sins, of the manifestations of our wretchedness? To ask oneself such a question is to overlook the central data in the problem and to turn on the one hand immanent Justice and the Law of equilibrium into a psychological contingency and on the other—since sin is minimized—human mediocrity into the measuring rod of the Universe. First of all, to speak of God 'punishing' is only a way of expressing a certain causal relationship; nobody would dream of accusing nature of meanness because the relationship of cause and effect is displayed in it according to the inherent logic of things: because for example, nettle seeds do not produce azaleas, or because, when a swing is pushed, a pendular and not an upward movement results. The good reason for the sanctions beyond death is apparent once we are aware of human imperfection; being a disequilibrium that imperfection ineluctably calls forth its own repercussion.[2] If the existence of

[1] Mazdeism formulated the problem of Omnipotence and of evil in a way which avoids the appearance of contradiction in the Divine Principle by opposing to Ahuramazda, or Ormuzd, the supreme and infinitely good God, a principle of evil, Auromainyu, or Ahriman, thus stopping short at a dualism which falls short of being metaphysically satisfactory, though admissible at a certain level of reality. The Buddhist formulation avoids the two dangers of contradiction in God Himself and of a fundamental dualism, but is obliged to sacrifice the personal aspect of God, at any rate in its general doctrine, and this makes it unassimilable for the majority of Occidentals and Semites.

[2] This is one meaning of Christ's saying that 'he who draws the sword shall perish by the sword' and also, though from a somewhat different point of view, of the saying that 'every house divided against itself shall fall'. This last saying is in particular applicable to the man who is unfaithful to his nature 'made in the image of God'.

creatures is really a proof of God for those who see through outward appearances, because manifestation is conceivable only in terms of a Principle (just as accidents have meaning only in relation to a substance) analogous things can be said about disequilibria: they presuppose an equilibrium which they have broken and they entail a concordant reaction, whether positive or negative.

To believe that man is 'all right', that he has the right simply to demand 'to be left alone', that he has no business with moral agitations and eschatological fears, means a failure to see that the limitations which in a sense define man have fundamentally a kind of 'abnormality'. The mere fact that we do not see what goes on behind our backs and are ignorant of what tomorrow will be like proves us to be in certain respects very insignificant and shows that we are 'accidents' of a 'substance' greater than ourselves, but shows at the same time that we are not the body and not of this world; neither this world nor our body is what we are. And here we would insert a parenthesis: if for thousands of years men could be content with the moral symbolism of recompense and punishment it is not because they were stupid (in which case their stupidity would have been infinite and incurable) but because they still preserved the sense of stability and instability, because they still had an innate feeling of real values in the case both of the world and of the soul. They had the certainty—and that in some degree through experience, since they were contemplative—on the one hand of divine norms and on the other of human imperfections; a symbolism was enough to recall to them that of which they already had a natural presentiment. A man spiritually perverted has, on the contrary, forgotten his initial majesty and the risks it involves; having no desire to occupy his mind with the fundamentals of his existence he believes that reality is incapable of recalling them to his mind. And the worst of all absurdities is to believe that the nature of things is absurd, for, were it so, whence could we draw light enabling us to recognize that it is so? Further, man is by definition intelligent and free: in practice he always remains convinced of this for at every opportunity he lays claim both to freedom and to intelligence: to freedom because he does not want to let himself be dominated, and to intelligence because he intends to be the judge of everything himself. But what decides our destiny in face of the Absolute

is our real nature and not our convenience, elevated to the
status of a norm; it may be that we want to desert our theomorphism while profiting from its advantages, but we cannot
escape the consequences that theomorphism implies. It is all
very fine for the modernists to despise what may seem to them
a disquiet, a feebleness or a 'complex' in traditional people;
their own way of being perfect is to ignore that the mountain is
crumbling whereas the apparent imperfection of those they
despise includes—or manifests—at any rate a serious possibility of escaping a cataclysm. And everything that has just
been said applies equally to whole civilizations: the traditional
civilizations include evils that can only be understood, or the
bearing of which can only be estimated, if regard is had to the
fact that these civilizations are based on certainty of the beyond
and, consequentially, on a corresponding indifference to transitory things. Conversely, in order rightly to evaluate the advantages of the modern world, and before seeing in it indisput-
able values, it must be borne in mind that these 'advantages'
are mentally conditioned by denial of the beyond and by the
cult of the things of this world.

Modern / traditional worlds comparison

Very many people today think in such terms as these: 'either
God exists, or He does not; if He exists and is what people say
He is, then He will recognize that we are good and do not
deserve punishment.' This means that they are prepared to
believe in His existence provided He conforms to their own
imaginings and recognizes the value they attribute to themselves. This is to forget, on the one hand that we cannot know
the standards by which the Absolute judges us, and on the
other that the 'fire' beyond the tomb is definitively nothing but
our own intellect actualized in opposition to our own falseness;
in other words it is the immanent truth breaking forth into the
full light of day. At death man is confronted by the unimaginable expanse of a reality no longer fragmentary but total, and
then by the norm of what he has pretended to be, because that
norm is part of Reality. Man therefore condemns himself;
according to the Quran it is his members themselves which
accuse him; once beyond the realm of lies his violations are
transformed into flames; nature, thrown out of balance and
falsified proves, with all its vain assurance, a shirt of Nessus.
It is not only for his sins that man burns; he burns too for his
majesty as an image of God. It is the preconceived idea of setting

up the fallen state as a norm and ignorance as a pledge of impunity which the Quran stigmatizes with vehemence—one might almost say by anticipation—by confronting the self-assurance of its contradictors with the terrors of the end of the world. This is indeed one of the most frequently recurring themes of this sacred Book, which sometimes marks by an almost despairing eloquence its character of being the final Message.

To sum up, the whole problem of guilt can be reduced to the relation between cause and effect. That man is far from being good is very amply proved both by ancient and by modern history: man does not have the innocence of animals; he is aware of his own imperfection, since the idea of that imperfection exists for him; thus he is responsible. What is called in moral terminology the fault of man and the chastisement of God is, in itself, nothing other than human disequilibrium coming into collision with the immanent Equilibrium; and this idea is of capital importance.

The notion of an 'eternal' hell, after having for many centuries stimulated fear of God and efforts towards virtue, has today rather the opposite effect and contributes to making the doctrine of the world beyond seem improbable; and, by a strange paradox, in a period which is one of contrasts and compensations, and at the same time generally speaking as refractory as it could be to pure metaphysic, only the esotericism of gnosis is in a position to render intelligible the very precariously held positions of exotericism and to satisfy certain needs of causality. Now the problem of divine punishment, which our contemporaries have such difficulty in admitting, can be summed up in two questions: first, is it possible for man who is responsible and free to oppose the Absolute either directly or indirectly, even if only in an illusory sense? Certainly he can, since the individual essence can be impregnated with any cosmic quality and there are consequently states that are 'possibilities of impossibility'.[1] And the second question is this:

[1] 'And they say: The Fire will not touch us save for a certain number of days. Say: Have ye received a covenant from Allah—truly Allah will not break His covenant—or tell ye concerning Allah that which ye know not? Nay, but whosoever hath done evil and his sin surroundeth him; such are the rightful owners of the Fire; they will abide therein' (khālidūn). (Quran, 11, 80-81). Here the whole emphasis is on the proposition: '. . . and his sin surroundeth him' (wa-ahātat bihi khatī 'atuhu), which indicates the essential, and so 'mortal' character of the transgression. This passage is a reply to men who believed, not that Hell as such is metaphysically limited, but that the duration of the punishment is equal to that of the sin.

can exoteric truth, for instance in regard to Hell, be total truth? Certainly not, since it is determined—in a certain sense 'by definition'—by a particular moral interest, or by particular reasons of psychological opportuneness. The absence of various compensating shades of expression in certain religious teachings can be explained in this way; the eschatologies relating to these religious perspectives are of course not antimetaphysical, but they are 'non-metaphysical' and anthropocentric,[1] and so much ? is this the case that in the context of these teachings certain truths appear 'immoral' or at least rather 'unseemly': it is therefore not possible for them to discern in infernal states aspects that are more or less positive, or the converse in paradisal states. By this we do not mean to say that there is symmetry as between Mercy and Rigour—the former has priority over the latter[2]—but rather that the relationship 'Heaven–hell' corresponds by metaphysical necessity to what is expressed in the Far-Eastern symbolism of the yin-yang in which the black portion includes a white point and the white portion a black point; if then there are compensations in gehenna because nothing in existence can be absolute and the divine Mercy penetrates everywhere,[3] there must also be in Paradise, not

---

[1] Theologians are not in principle unaware that the 'eternity' of hell—the case of paradise is somewhat different—is not on the same level as that of God and could not be identical with it; but this subtlety remains for them without consequences. If, in the Semitic Scriptures, exotericism is predicated by such ideas as creation *ex nihilo* and a survival both individual and eternal, the exoteric tendency likewise appears in Hindu and Buddhist Scriptures—though in a different fashion—in the sense that these texts appear to place on this earth those phases of transmigration which are neither celestial nor infernal; in the climate of Hinduism exotericism, always averse to subtle explanations, is reduced to simplicity of the symbols. Certainly one eschatology may be more complete than another, but none could be absolutely adequate by reason of the very limitation of human and earthly imagination.

[2] There is assymmetry as between celestial and infernal states because the former are eminently nearer to pure Being than the latter; their 'eternity' is thus on any reckoning different from that of the hells.

[3] El-Ghazzālī relates in his *Durrat el-fākhirah* that one man, when plunged into the fire, cried out more loudly than all the others: 'And he was taken out all burned. And God said to him: Why did you cry out more loudly than all the other people in the fire? He replied: Lord, Thou hast judged me, but I have not lost faith in Thy mercy. . . . And God said: Who despairs of the mercy of his Lord if not those who have gone astray? (Quran, XV, 56) Go in peace, I have pardoned you.' From a Catholic point of view this would refer to 'purgatory'. Buddhism knows of Bodhisattvas, such as Kshitigarbha, who give relief to the damned with celestial dew or bring them other alleviations, and this is an indication that there are angelic functions of mercy which reach even to hell.

indeed sufferings, but shadows bearing an inverse testimony to the same principle of compensation and signifying that Paradise is not God, as also that all existences are conjoined. Now this principle of compensation is esoteric—to make a dogma of it would be wholly contrary to the spirit of 'either . . . or' so characteristic of Western exotericism—and indeed we find Sufic writings giving expression to views remarkable for their shades of meaning: Jīlī, Ibn Arabī and others admit an aspect of enjoyment in the infernal state for, if on the one hand the man who has been reproved suffers from being cut off from the Sovereign Good and, as Avicenna emphasises, from deprivation of his earthly body although the passions subsist, on the other hand he remembers God, according to Jalāl ed-Dīn Rūmī, and 'nothing is sweeter than the remembrance of Allah'. Indeed in hell the wicked and the proud know that God is real, whereas on earth they either took no account of this or were always able to bring themselves to doubt it; thus something is changed in them by the mere fact of their death and this something is indescribable from the point of view of earthly life. 'The dead alone know the worth of life', say the Moslems. Here it is perhaps as well to recall also that those in hell would be *ipso facto* delivered if they had the supreme knowledge—of which they certainly possess the potentiality—so that even in hell they hold the key to their liberation; but what must above all be pointed out is that the second death referred to in the Apocalypse, as also the reservation expressed in the Quran where certain sayings about hell are followed by the phrase 'unless thy Lord wills otherwise' (*illā mā shā'a Llāh*),[1] indicate the point of

---

[1] (Surats VI, 129 and XI, 107). The same reservation concerns Paradise: ". . . they will abide there . . . so long as the heavens and the earth endure unless thy Lord willeth otherwise; a gift never failing' (XI, 108). This last proposition relates most directly to the participation by 'those brought nigh' (*muqarrabūn*) in the Divine Eternity by virtue of the supreme union; in their case (that of the *krama-mukti* of Vedantic doctrine) Paradise opens out into Divinity at the end of the cycle ('so long as the heavens and the earth endure'), as is also the case of the Paradises of Vishnu and of Amida. As for the reservation mentioned above, it indicates the possibility of later, though always beneficial changes for those who, to use a Sufi expression, 'prefer the garden to the Gardener'—those, that is, whose state is the fruit of action and not of knowledge or pure love. Here may also be mentioned the possibility of the Bodhisattvas who, while remaining inwardly in Paradise, enter a particular world which is by analogy 'earthly', and also, at a much lower level, those non-human benedictions which, thanks to a particular *karma*, a being may use up passively as a plant would. But none of this enters into the perspective of what are

intersection between the Semitic conception of perpetual hell and the Hindu and Buddhist conception of transmigration. In other words the hells are in the final count passages to individual non-human cycles and thus to other worlds.[1] The human state, or any other analogous 'central' state, is, as it were, surrounded by a ring of fire: in it there is only one choice, either to escape from 'the current of forms' upwards, towards God, or else to leave humanity downwards through the fire, the fire which is like the sanction of the betrayal on the part of those who have not realized the divine meaning of the human condition. If 'the human state is hard to obtain', as is held by Asiatic believers in transmigration, it is for the same reason of its centrality and theomorphic majesty equally hard to leave. Men go to the fire as being gods and they come out of the fire as being but creatures: God alone could go to hell eternally—if He could sin. Again: the human state is very near to the divine Sun, if we can at all speak of proximity in such a connection; the fire is the ultimate price—in reverse—of that privileged situation, how privileged can be gauged by the intensity and inextinguishability of the fire. From the gravity of hell we must infer the grandeur of man; we must not inversely infer from the seeming innocence of man the supposed injustice of hell.

What can to a certain extent excuse the common use of the word 'eternity' to designate a condition which is in Scriptural terms only a perpetuity[2]—the latter being only a 'reflection' of eternity—is the fact that analogically speaking ⟨eternity⟩ is a

called the monotheisms, a perspective which, moreover, does not include either the rhythm of the cosmic cycles or, *a fortiori*, the rhythm of the universal cycles (the 'lives of *Brahmā*'), although certain *ahadīth* and passages in the Bible (including, no doubt, the 'reign of a thousand years') refer to these ideas more or less overtly.

[1] According to the *Mānava-Dharma-Shāstra*, the *Mārkendeya Purāna* and other texts the transmigration of the 'damned' on their leaving hell begins by incarnations as lower animals. After all, the divine infinity requires that transmigration should take place in a 'spiroidal' mode: a being can never return to the same earth whatever the content of his new 'earthly' existence—an existence, that is to say, compounded of pleasure and suffering.

[2] 'The Greek word αἰώνιος really means "perpetual" and not "eternal", for it is derived from αἰών (the same word as the Latin *aevum*), which designates an indefinite cycle, and this is, moreover, also the primitive meaning of the Latin word *saeculum*, "age", by which it is sometimes translated' (R. Guenon: *Man and His Becoming According to the Vedanta*). In the same way, the 'beyond' of the Quran has the quality of an unlimited duration, or of immortality (*khuld*), or of a very long time (*abad, abadan*) and not that of eternity (*azal*).

closed circle, for here there is neither beginning nor end, whereas perpetuity is a circle with a spiral character and so open by very reason of its contingency. On the other hand what clearly shows the inadequacy of current belief in a survival that is both individual and eternal—this survival is inevitably individual in hell but not at the transpersonal peak of Felicity[1]—is the contradictory postulate it involves of an eternity with a beginning in time or of an act—and therefore a contingency—with an absolute consequence.

This whole problem of survival is dominated by two principles of truth: first, that God alone is absolute and that the relativity of cosmic states must consequently be manifested not only 'in space' but also 'in time', to use an analogy that is perhaps permissible; secondly, that God never promises more than He performs or never performs less than He promises—though He may always exceed His promises—and so the eschatological mysteries cannot give the lie to what the Scriptures say, though they can reveal things on which the Scriptures are silent in certain cases; 'and God is more wise' (*wa 'Llāhu a'lam*). From the point of view of transmigration the whole emphasis is on the idea that all that is not the Self or the Void is relative and it is added that what is limited in its fundamental nature must also be so in its destiny in some way or other,[2] so

[1] As El-Ghazzālī recalls in his *Ihya 'Ulūm ed-Dīn* the vision of God makes 'those who are brought nigh' (*muqqarabūn*) forget the houris and ends in the supreme union. Such too is the case of those who, having entered into the 'paradise of Amitabha', there achieve the realization of Nirvana, or in other words are reintegrated into the Principle at the great dissolution marking the end of the whole human cycle. '. . . On obtaining Deliverance the being is not "absorbed", though such may seem to be the case from the point of view of manifestation, for which the "transformation" appears to be a "destruction"; if one places oneself in the absolute reality, which alone remains for such a being, it is on the contrary expanded beyond all limits, if one can use such a figure of speech (which exactly translates the symbolism of steam from water spreading indefinitely in the atmosphere), since it has effectively realized the fullness of its possibilities.' (R. Guenon: op. cit. Chap. XX, end.) 'This is the state of abiding in Brahma. . . . He that has come to abide therein even at the end of life can attain to extinction in Brahma (*brahmanirvāna*).' (Bhagavadgītā, 11, 72)—If Nirvana is 'extinction' only in relation to the existential 'illusion', this 'illusion' is itself 'extinction' or 'void' in relation to Nirvana; as for him who enjoys this 'state'—if indeed such a term is still applicable—we must bear in mind the doctrine of the three simultaneous and hierarchically situated 'bodies' of the Buddhas: the earthly, the heavenly and the divine.

[2] None the less: 'O, Partha, neither here nor hereafter is there destruction for him; for none that does righteousness, my son, comes to evil estate.' (Bhagavadgītā VI, 40.) On this Shankara comments: 'He who has not succeeded in his yoga will not be subjected to an inferior birth.'

that it is absurd to talk of a state that is contingent in itself but delivered from every contingency in 'duration'. In other words, if the Hindu and Buddhist perspectives differ from that of monotheism, it is because, being centred on the pure Absolute[1] and on Deliverance, they underline the relativity of conditioned states and do not stop at these; they therefore insist on transmigration as such, the relative being then synonymous with movement and instability. At any spiritually normal period and in a setting that is traditionally homogeneous all these considerations on the different ways of looking at survival would be in practice superfluous or even harmful, and everything is, moreover, implicitly contained in certain Scriptural statements.[2] But for the world in dissolution in which we live it has become indispensable to show the meeting point where the divergences between Semitic and Western monotheism and the great traditions that originated in India are minimal or are resolved. It is true that such confrontations are rarely quite satisfactory in so far as they concern cosmology and every time precision is sought there is a risk of raising fresh problems; but these difficulties really only serve to show that we are here concerned with an infinitely complex domain which will never be adequately revealed to our earthly understanding. In a sense the Absolute is less difficult to 'grasp' than the tremendous abysses of Its manifestation.

There is another point which can hardly be over-emphasized. The monotheistic Scriptures, commonly so called, have no need to speak explicitly of certain seemingly paradoxical possibilities of survival given the perspective to which their providential field of expansion restricts them; their quality of *upāya* —of 'provisional and opportune truth'—obliges these Sacred Books to pass over in silence, not only the compensatory dimensions of the beyond, but also those prolongations which lie outside the 'sphere of interest' of the human being. It was in this sense that it was stated above that exoteric truth could only

[1] This is not merely a pleonasm, for the personal aspect of God is absolute in relation to man as such while being at the same time the first contingency in relation to the Self and—what amounts to the same thing—in respect of 'our' transontological intellect.

[2] In the case of Islam everything is strictly contained in the *Shahādah*, which provides a key to prevent any relativity whatever being set on the same level of reality as the Absolute. Other less fundamental formulas include more precise allusions.

be partial,[1] if we leave aside the polyvalence of its symbolism. The limiting definitions proper to exotericism are comparable to descriptions of an object of which only the form and not the colours can be seen.[2] 'Ostracism' of Sacred Scriptures is often a function of man's malice; the exotericism was efficacious so long as, despite everything, men still had a sufficient intuition of their own imperfection and of their ambiguous situation in face of the Infinite, but today everything is called in question, on the one hand by reason of the loss of this very intuition and on the other because of the inevitable encounters between very different religions, not to mention the scientific discoveries wrongly deemed capable of invalidating spiritual truths.

It should be clearly understood that Sacred Scriptures 'of the first rank' are never exoteric[3] in themselves,[4] whatever their expressions or their silences; they always leave a possibility of reconstituting the total truth (perhaps only from some minute element) which means that they always let it shine through them; they are never entirely compact crystallizations of partial perspectives.[5] This transcendence of the sacred Scriptures in

[1] The atrocities traditionally committed in the name of religion are a proof of this; in this respect only esotericism is beyond reproach. That there are necessary evils does not mean that they are blessings in the intrinsic sense of the word.

[2] There are *ahadīth* which occupy as it were an intermediate position between the two perspectives in question—the literal and the universal. For example: 'He (*Allāh*) will save men from hell when they are burned like charcoal.' Or again: 'By the God in whose hands is my soul, a time shall come when the gates of hell shall be closed and watercress (symbol of coolness) will grow on its soil.' Or: 'And God will say: the Angels, the Prophets and the believers have all interceded for sinners; now there remains none to intercede for them save the Most Merciful of the merciful (*arham er-rāhimīn*, God). And He will take a handful of fire and withdraw a people who never did any good.'—To this mercy in terms of time the Sufis, as we have seen, add a mercy in the very actuality of the state of those in hell.

[3] This reservation means that it is a question here of universal Revelations on which whole civilizations are founded and not of secondary inspirations destined for a particular school and having, for instance, a narrowly Vaishnava tendency.

[4] In their immediate sense they indubitably set out a 'dualistic' and anthropomorphic perspective with a limited eschatology; but, as Meister Eckhart has pointed out, every true meaning is a 'literal meaning'. According to a *hadīth nabawwī* (a saying of the Prophet himself) the verses of the Quran enclose, not merely an exoteric and an esoteric meaning, but also within the latter many other possible meanings, at least seven and at most seventy; their profusion has been compared to 'the waves of the sea'.

[5] 'Heaven and earth shall pass away, but my words shall not pass away', says the Gospel; and the Quran says: 'All things are ephemeral save the Countenance of *Allāh*.'

relation to their concessions to a particular mentality appears in the Quran notably in the form of the esoteric story of the meeting between Moses and El-Khidr. In this story we find, not only the idea that the point of view of the Law is always only fragmentary, though fully efficacious and sufficient for the individual as such—he being only a part and not a totality—but also the doctrine found in the Bhagavadgītā,[1] according to which neither good nor bad actions directly concern the Self; that is to say, only knowledge of the Self and, in terms of that knowledge, detachment in relation to action have absolute value, although it is clear that salvation in the most elementary sense can be obtained short of that value. Moses represents the Law, the particular and exclusive form, and El-Khidr universal Truth, which cannot be grasped from the standpoint of the 'letter', like the wind of which thou 'canst not tell whence it cometh, and whither it goeth'.

What matters for God as regards men is, not so much to supply scientific accounts of things that most men cannot understand, as to unleash a 'shock' through some symbolical concept; and that is precisely the role of the *upāya*. And in this sense the part played by the violent alternative 'Heaven-hell' in the consciousness of the monotheist is very instructive: the 'shock', with all it implies for man, reveals far more of the truth than some account that is 'more true' but less easily assimilated, less effective and so in practice 'more false' for a particular understanding. It is a matter of 'understanding', not with the brain alone, but with our whole being, and so also with our will; dogma is addressed to the personal substance rather than to thought alone, at any rate in cases where thought is liable to be only a superstructure; it speaks to thought only in so far as thought is capable of communicating concretely with our whole being, and in this respect men are not all the same. When God speaks to man He does not converse, He issues orders; He only wishes to instruct man in so far as He can change him: now ideas do not act in the same way on everyone, hence the diversity of the sacred doctrines. Those perspectives which are *a priori* dynamic—those of Semitic and Western monotheism—envisage the posthumous states, by a kind of compensation, in a static aspect, and thus as definitive; on the other hand those

[1] The Bhagavadgītā is like the 'Bible' of gnosis; and it is not without reason that Hindus often consider it as an Upanishad.

which are *a priori* static, which means more contemplative and less anthropomorphic—those of India and the Far East—view these states under an aspect of cyclic movement and cosmic fluidity. Or again; if the Semitic Occident represents the posthumous states as something definitive, it is implicitly correct in the sense that before us lie as it were two infinities, that of God and that of the macrocosm or of the incommensurable and indefinite labyrinth of the *samsāra*. In the last analysis it is this which is the 'invincible' hell and God who in reality is the positive and blissful Eternity; and if the perspective of Hinduism and of Buddhism insists on the transmigration of souls, that is, as has already been stated, because its profoundly contemplative character enables it not to limit itself to the human condition alone, and because on this account it inevitably underlines the relative and inconstant nature of all that is not the Absolute; for this perspective the *samsāra* can only be an expression of relativity. Whatever these divergences the meeting point between the different perspectives becomes visible in such concepts as 'the resurrection of the body', which is precisely a 're-incarnation'.

One other question which must also be answered here is the following, to which the Quran gives only an implicit answer: why is the universe made up on the one hand of worlds and on the other of beings which pass through these worlds? This is like asking why there is a shuttle passing through the warp, or why there is warp and weft, or again, why the same relationship of crossing is produced when a cross or a star is inscribed in a system of concentric circles, when, that is, the principle of weaving is applied in a concentric way. What we want to show is that, just as the relationship of centre to space cannot be conceived except in this form of the spider's web with its two modes of projection—one continuous and the other discontinuous—so the relationship of Principle to manifestation—which makes up the Universe—is only conceivable as a combination between worlds arranged according to gradation around the Divine Centre and beings who pass through them.[1] To speak of 'Existence' is to proclaim the relationship between receptacle and content, or between the static and the dynamic;

[1] The symbolism of the spider's web—the symbolism of cosmic compartments and their contents—is also to be found in Buddhist pictures of 'the Round of Existence'. The Quran is itself a picture of the cosmos: the surats are the worlds and the verses (*āyāt*) are the beings.

the journey of souls through life, death and resurrection is nothing other than the very life of the macrocosmos; even in our experience in this world we pass through days and nights, summers and winters; essentially we are beings who pass through states; and Existence is not to be conceived of otherwise. Our whole reality converges towards that unique 'moment' which alone matters: our meeting with the Centre. *Which is death?*

What was said above about divine sanctions and their root in human nature or its state of disequilibrium is equally applicable, from the point of view of their deep causes, to the calamities of this world and to death: both are alike explained by the necessity of a return shock after a loss of equilibrium.[1] The cause of death is the disequilibrium brought about by our fall and the loss of Paradise, and the trials of life arise, consequentially, from the disequilibrium of our personal nature. In the case of the gravest sanctions beyond the tomb this disequilibrium is in our very essence and reaches the point of an inversion of our theomorphism; man 'burns' because he does not want to be what he is—because he is free not to want to be it; and 'every house divided against itself shall fall'. From this it follows that every divine sanction is an inversion of an inversion, and since sin is an inversion in respect of the primordial equilibrium, we can speak of 'offences' committed against God, although very clearly there is no possible psychological meaning in the phrase despite (the inevitable anthropomorphism of exoteric conceptions) The Quran describes with the burning eloquence characterizing its last surats the final dissolution of the world; now all this can be transposed to the scale of the microcosm, in which death appears as the end of a world and as a judgment, as an absorption that is to say of the external by the internal in the direction of the Centre. When Hindu cosmology teaches that the souls of the dead go first of all to the Moon, it suggests indirectly, and aside from other far more important analogies, the experience of incommensurable solitude—'the terrors of death'—through which the soul passes 'against the grain' on leaving the protective matrix which the earthly world had been for it; the material moon is as it were

---

[1] According to the Quran all earthly ills 'come from yourselves' (*min anfusikum*), which does not mean that 'everything' does not 'come from God' (*kullum min 'indi 'Llāhi*).

the symbol of an absolute uprooting, of dark and sepulchral solitude, of the chill of eternity;[1] and it is this terrible *post mortem* isolation which marks the repercussion in relation not to some sin or other but to formal existence. At death all assurance and all competence fall away like a garment and the being who remains is impotent and like a lost child; nothing is left but a substance we have ourselves woven which may either fall heavily or on the contrary let itself be drawn up by Heaven like a rising star.[2]

Our existence as such is like a still innocent prefiguration of all transgression—innocent yet the generator of misery; at least it is so inasmuch as it is a demiurgic 'coming out' from the Principle, though not when regarded as a positive 'manifestation' of the Principle. If the *philosophia perennis* can combine the truth of Mazdean-Gnostic dualism with that of Semitic monism, the exotericisms for their part are forced to choose between a conception metaphysically adequate but morally contradictory and one that is morally satisfactory but metaphysically fragmentary. In the first case God is the cause of all: but then whence does evil come? In the second case evil comes from man: but then what is God?

One should never ask why misfortunes befall the innocent:

---

[1] In passing let it be said that it is this which raises doubts as to the psychological possibility of a journey into space. Even if we admit unforeseeable mental factors making such an adventure possible—and setting aside here the possibility of Satanic aid—it is very unlikely that on his return to earth a man would recover his former equilibrium and his old happiness. There is something analogous in lunacy, which is a breaking up or a decomposition, not of the immortal soul, but of its psychological habiliments, the empirical ego; lunatics are living-dead, most often a prey to dark influences but occasionally—in surroundings of great religious fervour—a vehicle on the contrary for some angelic influence, though in this case it is strictly speaking not really lunacy, the natural fissure being compensated, and in a way filled in, by heaven. In any case lunacy is characterized, especially as regards those who fall into it, if not always as regards those already in that condition, by an anguish marking the slipping down into an appalling sense of alienation, exactly as is the case at death, or, by hypothesis, during an interplanetary journey. In all these instances the normal limits of human surroundings are outpassed, and in a general sense this is equally true of modern science; it projects one into a void which leaves no choice but that of materialism or a metaphysical readaptation to which the very principles of that science are opposed.

[2] Red Indians put mocassins with embroidered soles on the feet of their dead and this is eloquently symbolical.

in the sight of the Absolute all is disequilibrium, 'God alone is good', and this truth cannot fail to be manifested from time to time in a direct and violent manner. If the good suffer, that means that all men would merit as much; old age and death prove it, for they spare no man. The sharing out of earthly good and ill fortune is a question of cosmic economy, although the immanent justice must also sometimes reveal itself in the light of day by showing the link between causes and effects in human action. Man's sufferings testify to the mysteries of his distance and separation, and they cannot not be, the world not being God.

But the levelling justice of death is infinitely more important for us than the diversity of earthly destinies. The experience of death resembles that of a man who has lived all his life in a dark room and suddenly finds himself transported to a mountain top; there his gaze would embrace all the wide landscape; the works of men would seem insignificant to him. It is thus that the soul torn from the earth and from the body perceives the inexhaustible diversity of things and the incommensurable abysses of the worlds which contain them; for the first time it sees itself in its universal context, in an inexorable concatenation and in a network of multitudinous and unsuspected relationships, and takes account of the fact that life had been but an 'instant', but a 'play'.[1] Projected into the absolute 'nature of things' man is inescapably aware of what he is in reality; he knows himself ontologically and without deforming perspective in the light of the normative 'proportions' of the Universe.

One of the proofs of our immortality is that the soul—which is essentially intelligence or consciousness—could not have an end that is beneath itself, in other words matter or the mental reflections of matter; the higher cannot be merely a function of the lower, it cannot be only a means in relation to what it surpasses. So it is intelligence in itself—and with it our freedom, which proves the divine range of our nature and our destiny. If we say that it 'proves' this, it is said unconditionally and without any wish to add any rhetorical precaution for the benefit of those myopic persons who imagine that they hold a

---

[1] According to a *hadīth* man sleeps and, when he dies, he awakes. But the gnostic ('*ārif*) is always awake, as the Prophet has said: 'my eyes slept, but my heart did not sleep'.

monopoly of the 'real' and the 'concrete'. Whether people understand it or not the Absolute alone is 'proportionate' to the essence of our intelligence; only the Absolute (*El-Ahad*, 'The One') is perfectly intelligible in the strict sense, so much so that it is only in It that the intelligence sees its sufficient reason and its end. The intellect, in its essence, conceives God because it is itself *increatus et increabile*; and thus and *a fortiori* it conceives or knows the meaning of contingencies; it knows the meaning of the world and the meaning of man. In fact the intelligence 'remembers' with the direct or indirect aid of Revelation. Revelation is the objectivation of the transcendent Intellect and to one degree or another 'awakens' the latent knowledge—or elements of knowledge—we bear in ourselves. Thus faith (in the wide sense, *imān*) has two poles, one 'objective' and 'external' and the other 'subjective' and 'internal': grace and intellection. And nothing is more vain than to raise in the name of the former a barrier of principle against the latter; the most profound 'proof' of Revelation—whatever its name—is Its eternal prototype which we bear in ourselves in our own essence.[1]

Like every Revelation the Quran is a flashing and crystalline expression of that which is 'supernaturally natural' to man's consciousness, that is, of our situation in the Universe, of our ontological and eschatological connections. It is for this reason that the Book of Allah is a 'discernment' (*furqān*), a 'warning' (*dhikrā*) and a 'light' (*nūr*) in the darkness of our earthly exile.

---

[1] This does not in any way profit rationalism or 'free-thinking', for the domain in which these operate is only a surface that has nothing to do with the transpersonal essence of the intelligence.

Chapter 3

The Prophet

To Europeans, and no doubt to most non-Moslems, Christ and the Buddha represent perfections that are immediately intelligible and convincing; we find this conviction reflected in the trinity put forward by Vivekananda—Jesus, the Buddha and Rāmakrishna—a trinity that is for several reasons inacceptable.[1] By contrast the Prophet of Islam seems complex and uneven and hardly compels recognition as a symbol except within his own traditional universe. The reason is that, unlike the Buddha and Christ, his spiritual reality is wrapped in certain human and earthly veils, and this because of his function as a legislator 'for this world'. He is thus akin to the other great Semitic Revealers, Abraham and Moses, and also to David and Solomon. From the Hindu point of view one could add that he is close to Rāma and Krishna whose supreme sanctity and saving power did not prevent the occurrence of all sorts of family and political vicissitudes. This allows us to bring out a fundamental distinction; there are not only those Revealers who represent exclusively 'the other world', there are also those whose attitude is at the same time divinely contemplative and humanly combative and constructive.

[1] It is inacceptable, first, because it is impossible in a truly Hindu perspective to put the Buddha and Christ in a trinity to the exclusion of Rāma and Krishna; secondly because Christ is foreign to India; thirdly, because, if non-Hindu worlds are taken into account, there is no reason for taking only Christ into consideration still, of course, from the point of view of Hinduism; fourthly, because there is no common measure between the river Ramakrishna and the oceans that were Jesus and the Buddha; fifthly, because Ramakrishna lived at a period in the cycle which could in any case no longer contain a plenary incarnation of the amplitude of the great Revealers; sixthly, because, in the Hindu system there is no room for another plenary and 'solar' incarnation of Divinity between the ninth and the tenth Avataras of Vishnu—the Buddha and the future *Kalki-Avatāra*. 'A single Prophet', such is the teaching of Et-Tahāwī, 'is more excellent than the whole number of all the friends of God', (the saints).

When one has acquired a real familiarity with the life of Muhammad according to the traditional sources[1] three elements stand out which could be provisionally designated by the following terms: piety, combativeness and magnanimity. By 'piety' is to be understood whole-hearted attachment to God, the sense of the beyond and absolute sincerity, and thus a characteristic found quite generally in saints and *a fortiori* in messengers of Heaven; it is mentioned because in the life of the Prophet it shows in particularly high relief, prefiguring in a sense the spiritual climate of Islam.[2]

Furthermore there were in his life wars and, detaching itself from this basis of violence, there was a superhuman grandeur of soul; there were also marriages and through them a deliberate entry into the earthly and social sphere—we do not say: into the worldly and profane sphere—and *ipso facto* an integration of collective human life into the spiritual realm in view of the Prophet's 'avataric' nature. On the plane of 'piety' attention must be drawn to the love of poverty, the fasting and the vigils; some people will no doubt object that marriage, and especially polygamy, are opposed to asceticism, but that is to forget, first, that married life does not remove the rigour of poverty, vigils and fasts, nor render them easy and agreeable,[3] and secondly, that in the case of the Prophet marriage had a spiritualized or 'tantric' character, as indeed has everything in the life of such a being because of the metaphysical transparency pheno-

---

[1] 'Traditional sources' because the profane biographers of the Prophet, whether Moslem or Christian, always seek to 'excuse' him, the former in a lay and anti-Christian sense and the latter, even in favourable cases, with a sort of psychological condescension.

[2] In the case of Christ and the Buddha one could not talk of manifestations of piety, that is to say of 'fear' and 'love'; the human is as it were extinguished in the divine message in conformity with the anthropotheism of the Christian and Buddhist perspectives.

[3] As regards Islam in general people too easily lose sight of the fact that the prohibition of fermented drinks unquestionably involved a sacrifice for the ancient Arabs and for the other peoples to be brought into Islam, all of whom knew wine. Nor is Ramadan a recreation, and the same is true of the regular, and often nocturnal, practice of prayer; most certainly Islam did not impose itself because it was easy. On his first visits to Arab towns the author was impressed by the austere and even sepulchral atmosphere: a kind of whiteness as of the desert was spread like a shroud over houses and people; everywhere there was a breath of prayer and of death. In this we see beyond question a trace of the soul of the Prophet.

mena then assume;[1] Looked at from outside, most of the
Prophet's marriages had, moreover, a 'political' aspect—
politics having here a sacred significance connected with the
establishing on earth of a reflection of the 'City of God'—and,
finally, Muhammad gave enough examples of long abstinences,
particularly in his youth when passion is considered to be most
strong, to be exempt from superficial judgments on this account.
Another reproach often levelled at him is that of cruelty; but it
is rather implacability that should be spoken of here, and it was
directed, not at enemies as such, but only at traitors, whatever
their origin; if there was hardness here, it was that of God
himself through participation in the Divine Justice which rejects and consumes. To accuse Muhammad of having a vindic-
tive nature would involve, not only a serious misjudgment of his
spiritual state and a distortion of the facts, but also by the same
token a condemnation of most of the Jewish Prophets and of the
Bible itself;[2] in the decisive phase of his earthly mission, at the
time of the taking of Mecca, the Messenger of Allah even showed
a superhuman gentleness in face of a unanimous feeling to the
contrary in his victorious army.[3]

At the beginning of the Prophet's career there were painful
obscurities and uncertainties, and these show that the mission
imposed on him arose, not from the human genius of Muhammad
—a genius which he himself never suspected—but essentially
from the divine choice; in an analogous way the seeming
imperfections of the great Messengers have always had a
positive meaning.[4] The complete absence in Muhammad of any
kind of ambition leads us moreover to make here a brief
digression; it is always astonishing to find that certain people,
strong in their purity of intention, in their talents and in their

[1] The *sunna* transmits this saying of the Prophet: 'I have never seen anything without seeing God in it', or, 'without seeing God nearer to me than it'.—
On the subject of sex see '*La Sagesse des Prophètes*' by Ibn Arabī, and especially
the chapters on Muhammad and Solomon, in the annotated translation by
Titus Burckhardt.

[2] All these considerations are adduced not to 'excuse imperfections' but
simply to explain facts. The Christian Church was also implacable—in the
name of Christ—at the period when it was still all-powerful.

[3] Among numerous manifestations of gentleness let just one *Hadīth* be
quoted: 'God has created nothing He loves better than the emancipation of
slaves, and nothing He hates more than divorce.'

[4] For instance, in the case of Moses, his difficulty in speaking indicated the
divine prohibition to divulge the mysteries.

combative power, imagine that God ought to make use of them, and wait impatiently, even with disappointment and bewilderment, for a call from Heaven to present itself or for some miracle; what they forget—and such forgetfulness is strange in defenders of spirituality—is that God has no need of any man and can well dispense with their natural endowments or their passions. Heaven only makes use of talents provided they have first been broken for God or else when a man has never been aware of them; a direct instrument of God is always raised from the ashes.[1]

Reference was made above to the 'avataric' nature of Muhammad, to which it might be objected that for Islam or, what comes to the same thing, by his own conviction Muhammad was not and could not be an Avatara; but this is not really the question because it is perfectly obvious that Islam is not Hinduism and notably excludes any idea of incarnation (hulūl); quite simply, and using Hindu terminology, which is the most direct or the least inadequate, we would reply that a certain Divine Aspect took on under particular cyclic circumstances a particular earthly form, something in full conformity with what the Envoy of Allah testified as to his own nature, for he said 'He who has seen me has seen God' (El Haqq, 'The Truth'); 'I am He and He is I, save that I am he who I am and He is He who He is'; 'I was a Prophet when Adam was still between water and clay' (before the creation); 'I have been charged to fulfil my mission since the best of the ages of Adam (the origin of the world), from age to age down to the age in which I now am'.[2]

[1] A 'direct instrument' is a man conscious of the part he has to play from the moment it is allotted to him; on the other hand anyone or anything can be an 'indirect instrument'.

[2] There is an Arabic saying that 'Muhammad is a mortal, but not as other mortals; (in comparison with them) he is like a jewel among pebbles'. Most profane critics have wrongly interpreted the reply: 'What am I, if not a mortal man and an Envoy?' (Quran, XVII, 93) given by the Prophet to unbelievers who asked him for absurd and out-of-place wonders as a denial of the gift of miracles, which Islam in fact attributes to all the prophets. Christ also refused to perform miracles when the tempter urged him to do so, setting aside here the intrinsic meaning of his answers. Muhammad's saying briefly means—in conformity with the perspective characterizing Islam, which emphasizes that every derogation of natural laws comes about 'with God's permission' (bi-idhni-'Llāh)—'What, if not a man like yourselves, am I apart from the Grace of God?' It should be added that the sunna bears witness to a number of miracles in the case of Muhammad which, as arguments to weaken (mu'jizāt) unbelief, are differentiated from the prodigies of the saints, which are called divine 'favours' (karāmāt).

In any case, if the attribution of divinity to an historical personage is repugnant to Islam, that is because its perspective is centred on the Absolute as such, as is shown for instance in the conception of the final levelling before the Judgment: God alone in this conception remains 'living' and all else is levelled in universal death including the supreme Angels, and so also even the 'Spirit' (*Er-Rūh*), the divine manifestation at the luminous centre of the cosmos.

It is natural that the upholders of Islamic exotericism (*fuqahā* or *'ulamā ezh-zhāhir* 'wise men of the outer order') should have an interest in denying the authenticity of those *ahādīth* which refer to the avataric nature of the Prophet, but the very concept of the 'Spirit of Muhammad' (*Rūh muhammadī*)—which is the Logos—proves the correctness of these *ahādīth*, whatever their historic value, even if it were admitted that this latter might be doubted. Each traditional form identifies its founder with the divine Logos and looks on the other mouth-pieces of Heaven, in so far as it takes them into consideration, as projections of this founder and as secondary manifestations of the one Logos; in the case of Buddhists, Christ and the Prophet can only be envisaged as Buddhas. When Christ says that 'no man cometh unto the Father but by me', it is the Logos as such who speaks although for the Christian world Jesus is truly identified with this one and universal Word.

The Prophet is the human norm in respect both of his individual and of his collective functions, or again in respect of his spiritual and earthly functions.

Essentially he is equilibrium and extinction: equilibrium from the human point of view and extinction in relation to God.

The Prophet is Islam; if Islam offers itself as a form of truth, of beauty and of power—and it is indeed these three elements which inspire it and which, on various planes, it tends by its very nature to actualize—the Prophet for his part incarnates serenity, generosity and strength. These virtues could also be enumerated in the inverse order according to the ascending hierarchy of their values and by reference to the levels of spiritual realization. Strength is the affirmation—which may at need be combative—of Divine Truth both in the soul and in the world, and here lies the distinction drawn in Islam between the two kinds of holy warfare, the greater (*akbar*) and the lesser (*aṣghar*), or the inner and the outer. Generosity compensates for the aggressive aspect of strength; it is charity and pardon.[1] These two complementary virtues of strength and generosity culminate, or are in a sense extinguished, in a third virtue, serenity, which is detachment from the world and from the ego, extinction in face of God, knowledge of the divine and union with it.

There is a certain, no doubt paradoxical, relationship between virile strength and virginal purity in the sense that both are concerned with the inviolability of the sacred,[2] strength in a dynamic and combative manner and purity in a static and defensive manner; it could also be said that strength, a 'warrior' quality, includes a mode or complement that is static or passive, and this is sobriety, love of poverty and of fasting and incorruptibility, all of which are 'pacific' or 'non-aggressive' qualities. In the same way generosity, which 'gives', has its static complement in nobility, which 'is'; or rather nobility is the intrinsic reality of generosity. Nobility is a sort of contemplative generosity; it is love of beauty in its widest sense: for the Prophet and for Islam it is here that aestheticism and love of cleanliness enter,[3] for the latter removes from things, and especially from the body, the mark of being earthly and fallen and so brings them back, both symbolically and in a certain manner even in virtuality, to their immutable and incorruptible prototypes, or to their essences. As for serenity, that also has a necessary complement in truthfulness which is as it were its active or discriminative aspect; it is the love of truth and of intelligence, so characteristic of Islam, and therefore it is also impartiality and justice. Now nobility compensates the aspect of narrowness in sobriety and these two complementary virtues find their culmination in truthfulness in the sense that they

[1] El-Ghazzālī says that the principle (*aṣl*) of all good actions (*mahāsīn*) is generosity (*karam*). *El Karīm* ('The Generous') is a Name of God.

[2] This is what is expressed by the 'illiteracy' of the Prophet (*el-ummī*, 'the unlettered'); Divine 'Science' can only be implanted in virgin soil. The purity of the Blessed Virgin is not unconnected with the sword of the archangel guarding the entrance to Paradise.

[3] The Prophet said that 'God detests dirtiness and uproar' and this is highly characteristic of the aspect of purity and calm in contemplation, an aspect which finds its reflection in Islamic architecture, ranging geographically speaking, from the Alhambra to the Taj Mahal. In the courtyards of mosques and palaces their calm and balance is echoed in the murmuring of the fountains, the undulatory monotony of which repeats that of the arabesques. For Islam architecture is, apart from calligraphy, the supreme sacred art.

subordinate themselves to it and, if need be, efface themselves or seem to do so, in its presence.[1]

The virtues of the Prophet form, so to speak, a triangle: serenity with truthfulness is the apex of the triangle and the two other pairs of virtues—generosity with nobility and strength with sobriety—form the base; the two angles of the base are in equilibrium and at the apex are reduced to unity. As was said above the soul of the Prophet is in its essence equilibrium and extinction.[2]

Imitation of the Prophet implies, first, strength as regards oneself, next, generosity as regards others and, thirdly, serenity in God and through God. It could also be said: serenity through piety, in the most profound sense of that term.

Such imitation moreover implies: first, sobriety in relation to the world; secondly, nobility within ourselves in our being; thirdly, truthfulness through God and in Him. But we must not lose sight of the fact that the world is also within us, and that, conversely, we are not other than the creation which surrounds us and, finally, that God created 'by the Truth' (bil-Haqq); the world is, both in its perfections and in its equilibrium, an expression of the Divine Truth.[3]

The aspect of 'force' is at the same time and indeed above all the active and affirmative character of the spiritual means or method; the aspect of 'generosity' is also the love of our immortal soul; while the aspect of 'serenity', which is, first, seeing all things in God, is also seeing God in all things. One may be serene because one knows that 'God alone is', that the world and all its troubles are 'non-real', but equally one may be serene because—admitting the relative reality of the world—

---

[1] The three virtues of strength, generosity and serenity, as well as the three other virtues, already find expression in the very sound of the words of the second testimony of faith (shahādah): *Muhammadun Rasūlu 'Llāh* (Muhammad is the Messenger of God).

[2] It would be wrong to seek to enumerate the virtues of Christ in this way for they cannot be said to characterize him, given that Christ manifests divinity and not human perfection, at any rate not expressly and explicitly so as to include also the collective functions of earthly man. Christ is divinity, love and sacrifice; the Virgin is purity and mercy. Similarly the Buddha could be characterized in the following terms; renunciation, extinction and pity, for it is indeed those qualities or attitudes which in a special sense he incarnates.

[3] An expression, that is to say, of the pure Spirit or, in Hindu terms, of pure 'Consciousness' (*Chit*) which objectifies itself in *Māyā* through Being (*Sat*).

one realizes that 'all things are willed by God', that the Divine Will acts in all things, that all things symbolize God in one or another respect and that symbolism is for God what might be called a 'manner of being'. Nothing is outside God; God is not absent from anything.

Imitation of the Prophet means actualizing a balance between our normal tendencies, or more exactly between our complementary virtues and, following from this and above all, it is extinction in the Divine Unity on the basis of this harmony. It is thus that the base of the triangle is in a certain sense absorbed into its apex, which appears as its synthesis and its origin or as its end and the reason for its existence.

If we now return to the description given above but formulate it somewhat differently, we can say that Muhammad is the human form orientated towards the Divine Essence; this 'form' has two chief aspects, corresponding respectively to the base and to the apex of the triangle, and these are nobility and piety. Now nobility is compounded of strength and generosity, while piety —at the level here in question—is compounded of wisdom and sanctity; it should be added that by 'piety' we must understand the state of 'spiritual servitude' ('ubūdiyah) in the highest sense of the term, comprising perfect 'poverty' (faqr, whence the word faqīr) and 'extinction' (fanā') before God, and this is not unrelated to the epithet 'unlettered' (ummī) which is applied to the Prophet. Piety is what links us to God; in Islam this something is, first of all an understanding, as deep as is possible, of the evident Divine Unity—for one who is 'responsible' must grasp this evidentness and there is here no sharp demarcation between 'believing' and 'knowing'—and next it is a realization of the Unity that goes beyond our provisional and 'unilateral' understanding which is itself ignorance when regarded in the light of plenary knowledge: there is no saint (wālī, 'representative', and so 'participant') who is not a 'knower through God' ('arif bil-Llāh). This explains why in Islam piety, and a fortiori the sanctity which is its flowering, has an air of serenity;[1] it is a piety of which the essence is that it opens out into contemplation and gnosis.

---

[1] It is on this account that some have reproached this piety with being 'fatalistic' or 'quietist'. The real tendencies in question in fact already show in the term 'islām', which means 'abandonment' (to God).

Or again, the phenomenon of Muhammad could be described by saying that the soul of the Prophet is made up of nobility and serenity, the latter comprising sobriety and truthfulness and the former strength and generosity. The Prophet's attitude to food and sleep is determined by sobriety and his attitude to woman by generosity; here the real object of generosity is the pole of 'substance' in humankind, this pole—woman—being envisaged in its aspect of being a mirror of the beatific infinitude of God.

Love of the Prophet constitutes a fundamental element in Islamic spirituality, although this love must not be understood in the sense of a personalistic *bhakti* which would presuppose divinizing the Prophet in an exclusive way.[1] It arises because Moslems see in the Prophet the prototype and model of the virtues which make the theomorphism of man and the beauty and equilibrium of the universe and are so many keys or ways towards the Unity which delivers, so that they love him and imitate him even in the very smallest details of daily life. The Prophet, like Islam as a whole, is as it were a heavenly mould ready to receive the influx of the intelligence and will of the believer and one wherein even effort becomes a kind of supernatural repose.

'Verily God and his angels bless the Prophet; Oh! Ye who believe bless him and give him salutation' (Quran, XXXIII, 56). This verse forms the scriptural foundation of the 'Prayer on the Prophet'—or more precisely the 'Blessing of the Prophet'—a prayer which is in general use in Islam because both the Quran and the *Sunna* recommend it, though it takes on a special character in esotericism where it becomes a basic symbol. The esoteric meaning of this verse is as follows: God, the Heaven and the Earth—or, the Principle (which is unmanifest), supraformal manifestation (the angelic states) and formal manifestation (comprising both men and the jinns, in other words the two

[1] By 'exclusive' is meant seeing the Divine in practice only in a human form and not apart from it as is the case in the cult of Rama or of Krishna. In this connection let us recall the analogy between the Hindu Avataras and the Jewish Prophets: the latter remained within the Judaic framework as did the former within the Hindu framework save for one single great exception in each case: Buddha and Christ. David brought the Psalms and Solomon the Song of Songs, as Rāma inspired the *Rāmāyana* and the *Yoga-Vasishta* (or *Mahārā-māyana*) and Krishna the *Mahābhārata*, including the *Bhagavad Gītā*, and also the *Śrīmad Bhāgavatam*.

categories of corruptible beings,[1] whence the need for an injunction)—confer (or transmit as the case may be) vital graces on universal Manifestation, or, in another respect, on the centre of that Manifestation, namely the cosmic intellect.[2] One who blesses the Prophet blesses by implication the world and the universal Spirit (*Er-Rūh*),[3] the Universe and the Intellect, both the Totality and the Centre, so that the blessing, multiplied tenfold, comes back from each of these manifestations of the Principle[4] on him who has truly put his heart into this prayer.

The terms of the 'Prayer on the Prophet' are generally as follows, though there are many variants and developments of it: 'Oh, (my) God (*Allahumma*), bless our Lord Muhammad, Thy Servant (*'Abd*) and Thy Messenger (*Rasūl*), the unlettered Prophet (*En-Nabī el-ummī*), and his family and his companions, and salute them.' The words 'salute' (*sallam*), 'salutation' (*taslīm*) or 'peace' (*salām*)[5] signify a reverential homage on the part of the believer (the Quran says: 'And give him greeting' or 'salutation') and thus a personal attitude, whereas the blessing brings in the Divinity, for it is He who blesses; on the part of

---

[1] These are the two 'weights' or 'species having weight' (*eth-thalaqān*) of which the Quran speaks in the Surat of the Merciful, verse 31. Men are created of 'clay' (*tin*), that is of matter, and the jinns of 'fire', or an immaterial, animic or, as the Hindus would say, 'subtle' (*sukshma*) substance. As for the angels, they are created of 'light' (*nūr*), of a supra-formal substance; the differences between angels are like those between colours, sounds or perfumes, not those between forms, which to them appear as petrifactions and fragmentation.

[2] This prayer is thus at least partly equivalent to the Buddhist good wish 'May all beings be blissful!'

[3] Also called the 'First Intellect' (*El-'Aql el-awwal*); it is either 'created' or 'uncreated' according to the way it is envisaged.

[4] The Prophet said: 'He who blesses me once shall be ten times blessed by God. . . .' Another *hadīth* says: 'Truly the Archangel Gabriel came to me and said: "Oh Muhammad, none of thy community shall bless thee without my blessing him ten times and none of thy community shall greet thee without my greeting him ten times".' According to another *hadīth* from every prayer of the Prophet God created an angel, and this is full of meaning from the point of view of the economy of spiritual and cosmic energies. Regular readers of the author's works are already familiar with the following Vedantic classification, also found in the writings of René Guénon: gross or 'material' manifestation and subtle or 'animic' manifestation, these two together constituting manifestation with form; formless (supra-formal) or 'angelic' manifestation, which together with manifestation with form makes up manifestation as such; and finally, the unmanifest which is the Principle and comprises both Being and Non-Being (or Beyond-Being). The basis of these categories is the primary distinction between the Principle and manifestation.

[5] In Arabic to salute or greet means 'to give peace'; the words: 'Peace be with you' (*es-salāmu 'alaikum*) are spoken.

God 'salutation' is a 'look' or a 'word', that is to say an element of grace, which is not 'central' as in the case of the 'blessing' (*salāt*: *sallā 'alā*, 'pray on') but 'peripheric' and so relating to the individual and to life, not to the intellect and to gnosis. That is why the Name of Muhammad is followed by both 'blessing' and 'salutation' whereas the names of the other divine 'Messengers' and of the Angels are followed only by the 'salutation': from the point of view of Islam it is Muhammad who 'actually' and 'definitively' incarnates the Revelation, and Revelation corresponds to the 'blessing' not to the 'salutation': in the same more or less exoteric sense it could be said that the 'blessing' refers to the prophetic inspiration and to the 'relatively unique' and 'central' character of the Avatara envisaged, while the 'salutation' refers to the human, cosmic and existential perfection common to all the Avataras or to the perfection of the Angels.[1] The 'blessing' is a transcendent, active and 'vertical' quality whereas the 'salutation' is an immanent, passive and 'horizontal' quality: again, the 'salutation' concerns the 'exterior', the 'support', whereas the 'blessing' concerns the 'interior' or the 'content' whether in the case of divine acts or of human attitudes. Herein lies the whole difference between the 'supernatural' and the 'natural': the 'blessing' signifies the divine presence inasmuch as it is a continual influx, which in the microcosm—in the Intellect—becomes intuition or inspiration and, in the case of the Prophet, Revelation; on the other hand the 'peace' or 'salutation' signifies the divine presence inasmuch as it is inherent in the cosmos, becoming, in the microcosm, intelligence, virtue and wisdom; it concerns the existential equilibrium, the cosmic economy. It is true that intellective inspiration—or innate knowledge—is equally 'supernatural', but it is so, as it were, in a 'natural' manner within the framework and in accordance with the possibilities of 'Nature'.

According to the Shaikh Ahmed El-Allawi the divine act (*tajallī*) expressed by the word *sallī* ('bless') is like lightning, instantaneous in mode, and includes the extinction in some

---

[1] The Spirit (*Er-Rūh*) is here an exception because of its central position among the Angels which confers on it the 'Prophetic' function in the highest sense; the Quran mentions it separately from the angels and it is also said that the Spirit was not required to prostrate before Adam as they were; in Moslem logic he would merit, like Muhammad, both the *salāt* and the *salām*. The Archangel Gabriel is a personification of a function of the Spirit, the celestial ray which strikes the Prophets on earth.

degree of the human receptacle submitted to it, whereas the divine act expressed by the word *sallim* ('salute') spreads the divine presence in the modalities of the very individuality; the Shaikh said this is why the *faqīr* should always ask for *salām* ('peace') which corresponds to the divine 'Salutation'[1] in order that revelations or intuitions should not vanish like flickers of lightning but become fixed in his soul.

In the verse of the Quran which instituted the blessing of Muhammad it is said that 'God and His angels bless the Prophet', but the 'salutation' is only mentioned at the end of the verse, where it is a question of the believers; the reason for this is that the *taslīm* (or *salām*) is here taken to be understood, which means that at root it is an element of the *ṣalāt* and is only dissociated from it *a posteriori* in relation to the contingencies of the world.

The initiatic aim of the 'Prayer on the Prophet' is the aspiration of man towards his totality. Totality is that of which we are a part; and we are a part, not of God who is without parts, but of Creation, which, taken as a whole, is the prototype and norm of our being, while its centre, *Er-Rūh*, is the root of our intelligence, this root is a vehicle for the 'Uncreated Intellect', *increatus et increabile* according to Meister Eckhart.[2] The totality is perfection while the part as such is imperfect, for it manifests a rupture of the equilibrium of existence and so of the totality. In the sight of God we are 'nothing' or 'everything' according to the point of view[3] but we are never 'a part'; we are, on the other hand, a part in relation to the Universe, which is the archetype, the norm, equilibrium, perfection; it is 'Universal Man' (*El-Insān el-Kāmil*)[4] of which the human manifestation is the Prophet, the Logos, the Avatara. The Prophet—envisaged in the esoteric and universal meaning of the term—is thus the totality of which we are a fragment; but

[1] And this is precisely what he does through the 'Prayer on the Prophet'.

[2] According to the perspective of unity of essence this root is also identifiable with the 'Uncreated Intellect'.

[3] 'Nothing' from the ordinary 'separative' point of view, and 'everything' from the 'unitive' point of view, that of the 'oneness of the Real' (*Wahdat El-Wujūd*).

[4] Cf. *De l'homme Universel* by 'Abd El-Karīm-Jīlī (translated and commentated by Titus Burckhardt).

this totality is also manifested in us and that in a direct manner;
it is the intellectual centre, 'the eye of the heart', the seat of the
'Uncreated', the celestial or divine point in relation to which
the ego is the microcosmic periphery;[1] thus we are peripheric in
relation to the Intellect (*Er-Rūh*) and a part in relation to
Creation (*El-Khalq*). The Avatara represents both these poles
at once; he is our totality and our centre, our existence and our
knowledge; the 'prayer on the Prophet'—like every analogous
formula—has consequently not only the sense of an aspiration
towards our existential totality, but also by that very fact the
sense of an 'actualization' of our intellectual centre, these two
points of view being moreover inseparably linked together. Our
movement towards the totality—a movement the most elementary expression of which is charity in the sense of the
abolition of the illusory and passional division between 'I' and
'other than I'—at the same time purifies the heart, or in other
words frees the intellect from the obstructions standing in the
way of unitary contemplation.

In the blessing of Muhammad—the 'prayer on the Prophet'—
the epithets applied to the Prophet apply equally—or even
more—to the Totality and the Centre of which Muhammad is
the human expression, or rather 'an expression' if we take into
account the whole of humanity in all places and at all periods.
The name Muhammad itself means the 'Glorified' and indicates
the perfection of Creation, affirmed also in Genesis in the words:
'And God saw that it was good'; moreover the words 'our Lord'
(*Seyyidunā*) used before the name Muhammad indicate the
primordial and normative quality of the Cosmos in relation to
ourselves.

The epithet following the name of Muhammad in this prayer
is 'Thy servant' ('*abduka*): the Macrocosm is the 'servant' of
God because manifestation is subordinate to the Principle, or
the effect to the Cause; Creation is 'Lord' in relation to man and
'Servant' in relation to the Creator. Thus the Prophet is—like
Creation—essentially an 'isthmus' (*barzakh*), a 'line of demarca-

---

[1] In the same way the lotus on which the Buddha is enthroned is both the
manifested Universe and the heart of man, each of these being envisaged as
a support of Nirvana. In the same way too the Blessed Virgin is both pure
universal Substance (*Prakriti*), the matrix of the manifested divine Spirit
and of all creatures in respect of their theomorphism, and the primordial
substance of man, his original purity, his heart inasmuch as it is the support
of the Word which delivers.

tion' and at the same time a 'point of contact' between two degrees of reality.

Next comes the epithet 'Thy Messenger' (rasūluka): this attribute concerns the Universe inasmuch as it transmits the possibilities of Being to its own parts—to the microcosms—through the medium of the phenomena or symbols of nature; these symbols are the 'signs' (āyāt) spoken of in the Quran,[1] the proofs of God which the Sacred Book recommends for meditation by those 'endowed with understanding'.[2] The possibilities thus manifested transcribe in the 'external' world the 'divine truths' (haqā'iq) just as intellectual intuitions and metaphysical concepts transcribe them in the human subject; the Intellect, like the Universe, is 'Messenger', 'Servant', 'Glorified' and 'our Lord'.

The 'Prayer on the Prophet' sometimes includes the following two attributes: 'Thy Prophet' (Nabīyuka) and 'Thy Friend' (Habībuka); this second qualification expresses intimacy, the generous proximity—not the opposition—between manifestation and the Principle; as for the word 'Prophet' (Nabī), this indicates a 'particular message', not the 'universal message' of the 'Messenger' (Rasūl):[3] in the world it stands for the whole collection of cosmic determinations concerning man including natural laws; and within ourselves it is awareness of our latter end together with all that implies for us.

As for the next epithet, 'the unlettered Prophet' (En-Nabī el-ummī), this expresses the 'virginity' of the receptacle, whether universal or human; in respect of inspiration it is determined by nothing except by God; before the Divine Pen it is a blank page; none but God fills the Creation, the Intellect, the Avatara.

---

[1] It has already been pointed out that the word 'sign', when it does not relate to phenomena of this world, is applied to the verses of the Quran, and this clearly shows the analogy between Nature and Revelation.

[2] It is therefore quite possible for a tradition to be founded wholly on this symbolism; this is especially true of Shinto and of the tradition of the sacred pipe among the North American Indians.

[3] The Nabī is such not because he receives and transmits a particular message, one, that is, limited to particular circumstances, but because he possesses nubuwwah, the mandate of prophecy; every Rasūl is a Nabī, but not every Nabī is a Rasūl; it is somewhat like saying that every eagle is a bird, but not every bird an eagle. The meaning 'particular message' is called for, not just by the fact that the man is a Nabī, but by the fact that he is so without being a Rasūl. It is as a Nabī and not as a Rasūl that Muhammad is 'unlettered', just as—to return to our comparison above—it is because it is a bird that the eagle can fly, not because it is an eagle.

The 'blessing' and the 'salutation' are applied, not only to the Prophet, but also to 'his family and his companions' ('alā ālihi wa-sahbihi), that is, in the macrocosmic order, to Heaven and earth or to supra-formal and formal manifestation, and, in the microcosmic order, to soul and body, the Prophet being in the first case the Divine Spirit (Er-Rūh) and in the latter the Intellect (El-'Aql) or the 'Eye of the Heart' ('Ayn el-Qalb); Intellect and Spirit coincide in their essence in that the former is like a ray of the latter. The Intellect is the 'Spirit' in man; the 'Divine Spirit' is nothing other than the universal Intellect.

The epithets applied to the Prophet mark the spiritual virtues, the chief of which are: 'poverty' (faqr, which is a quality of the 'abd)[1] next 'generosity' (karam, a quality of the Rasūl)[2] and finally 'truthfulness' or 'sincerity' (sidq, ikhlās, a quality of the Nabī el-ummī).[3] 'Poverty' is spiritual concentration, or rather its negative and static aspect, non-expansion, and consequently 'humility' in the sense of the 'cessation of the fire of the passions' (in the words of Tirmīdhī); as for 'generosity', it is akin to 'nobility' (sharaf); it is the abolishing of egoism and this implies 'love of one's neighbour' in the sense that the passional distinction between 'I' and 'other' is outstripped; finally 'truthfulness' is the contemplative quality of the intelligence and, on the plane of reason, is logic or impartiality, in a word 'love of truth'.

From the initiatic point of view the 'Prayer on the Prophet' relates to the 'intermediate stage' to the 'expansion' which follows 'purification' and precedes 'union'; herein lies the deepest meaning of the hadīth: 'No man will meet God who has not first met the Prophet.'[4]

The 'Wheel' Analogy

The 'Prayer on the Prophet' can be likened to a wheel; the vow of blessing is its axle; the Prophet is its hub; his family make up the spokes; his Companions are the rim.

[1] In the sense that the 'abd has nothing that belongs to him as his own.

[2] The Rasūl is indeed a 'mercy' (rahmah): he is disinterestedness itself, the incarnation of charity.

[3] Truthfulness is inseparable from virginity of spirit in the sense that the spirit must be free from all artifice, from all prejudice and from any passional interference.

[4] This is also the initiatic meaning of the saying in the Gospels: 'No man cometh unto the Father, but by me.' None the less the difference of 'accent' which distinguishes the Christian perspective from Sufism must be taken into account.

In the widest interpretation of this prayer the blessing corresponds to God, the name of the Prophet to the universal spirit,[1] the Family to the beings who participate in God—through the Spirit—in a direct manner, and the Companions to those beings who participate in God indirectly but likewise thanks to the Spirit. This extreme limit can be defined in various ways according to whether we envisage the Moslem world, or the whole of humanity, or all creatures on earth, or even the whole Universe.[2]

The individual will, which is both egocentric and dispersed, must be converted to the universal Will which is 'concentric' and transcends earthly humanity.

As a spiritual principle the Prophet is not only the Totality of which we are separate parts or fragments, he is also the Origin in relation to which we are so many deviations;[3] in other words the Prophet as Norm is not only the 'Whole Man' (al-Insān-el-Kāmil) but also the 'Ancient Man' (el-Insān el-Qadīm). Here there is a sort of combination of a spatial with a temporal symbolism; to realize the 'Whole' or 'Universal' Man means to come out from oneself, to project one's will into the absolutely 'Other', to extend oneself into the universal life which is that of all things; while to realize the 'Ancient' or 'Primordial' Man means to return to the origin which we bear within us; it means to return to eternal childhood, to rest in our archetype, in our primordial and normative form, or in our theomorphic substance. According to the spatial symbolism the way towards realization of the 'Whole Man' is height, the ascending vertical which expands into the infinity of Heaven; according to the temporal symbolism the way towards the 'Ancient Man' is the past in a quasi-absolute sense, the divine and eternal origin.[4] The 'Prayer on the Prophet' relates to the

[1] Er-Rūh, which includes the four archangels; on the earthly plane and in the Moslem cosmos it is the Prophet and the four first Caliphs.

[2] The symbolism of the Prayer on the Prophet closely corresponds to that of the Tibetan prayer-wheels: a prayer, inscribed on a band of paper, blesses the world by its rotation.

[3] It is in this sense that, according to St Bernard, our ego should seem to us 'something to be despised' and that, according to Meister Eckhart, one must 'hate one's soul'.

[4] This throws a revealing light on the meaning of tradition as such and also in a more particular sense on the cult of ancestors.

spatial symbolism in the epithet *Rasūl*, 'Messenger'—though here the dimension is designated in a descending direction— and to the temporal symbolism in the epithet *Nabī el-ummī*, 'unlettered Prophet', which clearly is connected with the origin.

The term 'the Ancient Man' thus more particularly refers to the Intellect, to perfection of 'consciousness', and the term 'the Whole Man' to existence, to perfection of 'being'; but at the same time on the plane of the spatial symbolism itself the centre refers to the Intellect, whereas on the plane of the temporal symbolism duration refers to Existence, for it extends indefinitely. We can establish a connection between the origin and the centre on the one hand and between duration and the totality—or limitlessness—on the other; it could even be said that the origin, which in itself cannot be grasped, is for us situated at the centre and that duration, which everywhere eludes us, coincides for us with totality. In the same way, starting from the idea that the 'Whole Man' particularly concerns the macrocosm and the 'Ancient Man' the microcosm, it could be said that in its totality the world is Existence, whereas in origin the human microcosm is Intelligence, though only in a sense since we do not go beyond the realm of the created and of contingencies.

On the plane of the 'Whole Man' two dimensions can be distinguished: 'Heaven' and 'Earth', or 'height' (*tūl*) and 'breadth' (*'ardh*): 'height' links the earth to Heaven, and, in the case of the Prophet, this link is the aspect of *Rasūl* ('Messenger' and so also 'Revealer') while the earth is the aspect of *'Abd* ('Servant'). These are the two dimensions of charity: love of God and love of the neighbour in God.

On the plane of the 'Ancient Man' we shall not distinguish two dimensions for, in the origin, Heaven and Earth were one; as we have already seen, this plane is related to the 'unlettered Prophet'. His virtue is humility or poverty: to be only what God has made us, to add nothing; pure virtue is apophatic.

Let us sum up this doctrine as follows: the nature of the Prophet comprises the two perfections of totality[1] and of origin.[2] Muhammad incarnates the theomorphic and harmonious

---

[1] 'God said: Oh Adam! Cause them to know their names!' (Quran, II, 33)— 'And when We said to the angels: Prostrate yourselves before Adam!' (Quran, II, 34).

[2] 'Assuredly we have created man in the most fair form.' (Quran, XCV, 4).

totality[1] of which we are fragments and also the origin in relation to which we are states of decay, in each case when considered as individuals. For the Sufi, to follow the Prophet means extending the soul to the life of all beings, 'to serve God' (*'ibādah*) and to 'pray' (*dhakara*) with all and in all;[2] but it also means reducing the soul to the 'divine remembering' (*dhikru 'Llāh*) of the one and primordial soul;[3] in the final analysis and through the various poles envisaged—the poles of totality and origin, of plenitude and simplicity—it means realizing both the 'Infinitely Other' and the 'Absolutely Oneself'.

The Sufi, after the pattern of the Prophet, wants neither 'to be God' nor 'to be other than God': and this is not unconnected with all that has been said above, and with the distinction between 'extinction' (*fanā*) and 'permanence' (*baqā*). There is no extinction in God without Universal charity and there is no permanence in Him without that supreme poverty which is submission to the origin. As we have seen the Prophet represents both universality and primordiality, just as Islam in its deepest meaning is 'that which is everywhere' and 'that which has always been'.

Taken as a whole these considerations enable us to understand how greatly the Islamic way of envisaging the Prophet differs from the Christian or Buddhist cults. The sublimation of the Prophet is effected, not by starting out from the idea of an earthly divinity, but by means of a kind of metaphysical mythology; Muhammad is either man among men—we do not say 'ordinary man'—or Platonic idea, cosmic and spiritual symbol, unfathomable Logos;[4] never is he God incarnate.

---

[1] These two qualities are essential. The creation is 'good' because it is made in the image of God and because it compensates disequilibria—which are ontologically necessary else they would not exist—by the total equilibrium, which indirectly 'transmutes' them into factors of perfection.

[2] 'The seven Heavens and the earth and those in them praise Him; and there is nothing that does not chant His praises, but ye understand not their song. . . .' (Quran, XVII, 44).

[3] 'And every time they shall receive a fruit (in Paradise) they shall say: this is what we have received aforetime. . . .' (Quran, II, 25).

[4] It is said that, without Muhammad, the world would not have been created; thus he is indeed the Logos, not as man, but in his 'inner reality' (*haqīqah*) and as the 'Muhammadan Light' (*Nūr muhammadiyah*). It is also said that the virtues of the Prophet are created, since they are human, but

The Prophet is above all a synthesis combining human 'littleness' with the divine mystery. This aspect of being a synthesis, or a reconciliation of opposites, is characteristic of Islam and expressly results from its being the 'last Revelation'. If the Prophet is the 'Seal of Prophecy' (*khātam en-nubuwwah*) or of 'the Messengers' (*el-mursalīn*), this implies that he should appear as a synthesis of all that came before him; hence his aspect of 'levelling', that something 'anonymous' and not to be numbered, which is apparent also in the Quran.[1] Those who, by reference to the example of Jesus, find Muhammad too human, are following a line of reasoning just like that of those who, by reference to the extremely direct spirituality of the *Bhagavad-gītā* or the *Prajnā-pāramita-hridaya Sūtra*, would consider the Bible 'too human' to have any title to the dignity of the divine Word.

The virtue, claimed by the Quran, of being the last Revelation and the synthesis of the prophetic cycle reveals itself, not only in the external simplicity of a dogma which is inwardly open to every degree of profundity, but also in the capacity Islam has of integrating all men as it were into its centre, of conferring on all the same unshakeable and if need be combative faith and of making them participate at least virtually though effectively in the half-celestial, half-earthly nature of the Prophet.

that they are 'none the less eternal in so far as they are qualities of Him of whom eternity is the attribute' (according to *El-Burdah* by the Shaikh El-Buṣīrī); in the same way the Prophet is named '*Haqq* (Truth)' while *El-Haqq* ('The Truth') is a divine Name. The *haqīqah* of Muhammad is described as 'a mystery'; it is either hidden or blindingly bright and can only be interpreted from afar.

[1] Aïshah, the 'favourite wife' of Muhammad, said that the Quran reflects or prefigures the soul of God's Messenger.

Chapter 4

The Way

IN this section our aim is not so much to treat of Sufism exhaustively or in detail—other writers have had the merit of doing this with varying degrees of success—but rather to envisage the Way (*tarīqah*) in its general aspects or in its universal reality; therefore the terms used will not always be those peculiar to Islam. Now, when envisaged in a very general manner, the ~~Way presents itself first of all as the polarity of 'doctrine' and 'method', or as metaphysical truth accompanied by contemplative concentration~~; in short everything in it is reducible to these two elements: intellection and concentration or discernment and union. For us, who are in the realm of relativity since we exist and think, metaphysical truth is in the first place discrimination between the Real and the unreal or 'less real'; and concentration or the operative act of the spirit—prayer in its very widest sense—is in a way our response to the truth which offers itself to us; it is Revelation entering into our consciousness and becoming in some degree assimilated by our being.

~~For Islam, or to be more precise for Sufism which is its kernel,~~[1] the metaphysical doctrine is—as we have many times pointed out—that 'there is no reality save the One Reality' and that, in so far as we are obliged to take account of the existence of the world and of ourselves, 'the cosmos is the manifestation

---

[1] We would not wish to attribute to a religious faith as such sapiential theses which it can only enunciate by implication. For the 'science of religions' esotericism comes after dogma, of which it is supposed to be an artificial development and even one borrowed from extraneous sources: in reality the sapiential element must precede the exoteric formulation since it is the former which, being a metaphysical perspective, determines the form. Without a metaphysical foundation there can be no authentic religion; doctrinal esotericism is only the development, starting from the Revelation itself, of what 'existed from the beginning'.

of Reality.'[1] Vedantists, we repeat, say that 'the world is false; Brahma is true', but 'all things are *Atmā*'; all eschatological truths are contained within this second statement. It is by virtue of this second truth that we are saved; according to the first we even 'are not' although we do 'exist' in the field of the reverberations of the contingent. It is as if we were saved beforehand because we are not and because 'naught shall subsist save the Countenance of God'.

The distinction between the Real and the unreal coincides in a sense with that between Substance and accidents; the Substance-accident relationship makes it easy to understand the 'less real or unreal' nature of the world and reveals to those capable of grasping it the inanity of the error which attributes an absolute character to phenomena. Moreover the common meaning of the word 'substance' clearly shows that there are intermediate substances which are 'accidental' by comparison with pure Substance but none the less play the part of substances in relation to what is for them accidental: these substances are, in ascending order, matter, aether, the life-substance, supra-formal and macrocosmic substance—which could also be termed 'angelic'—and finally universal, meta-cosmic Substance which is one of the poles of Being, or is its 'horizontal dimension' or feminine aspect. The antimetaphysical error of the *asūras* is that they take accidents for reality and deny Substance by describing it as unreal or abstract.[2]

Being is the 'Relative Absolute', or God as 'relatively absolute', that is to say in so far as He creates. The pure Absolute does not create; in order to introduce here the ideas of 'Substance' and 'accidents' one would have to think of the essential divine qualities arising out of Beyond-Being, or out of the Self and crystallizing in Being, but such an application would none the less be inadequate.

To perceive the unreality—or the lesser or relative reality—of the world means at the same stroke to perceive the symbolism of phenomena; to know that the 'Substance of substances' is alone absolutely real, or that it is strictly speaking the only

---

[1] The cosmos in the perfection of its symbolism, Muhammad; here the reader will recognize the second *Shahādah*.

[2] We believe the attribution to Heracleitus of the modern 'actualism' (Aktualitäts-Theorie) to be mistaken, since a theory of the cosmic play of the All-Possibility is not necessarily a materialistic pantheism.

Accidents as transitory things (?)

reality, means to see Substance in and through every accident; thanks to this initial knowledge of Reality the world becomes metaphysically 'transparent'. When it is said that a Bodhisattva sees only space and not its contents, or that he looks on the latter as being space, this means that he sees only Substance, which in relation to the world appears as a 'void' or, contrariwise, that the world appears as a 'void' in terms of the principial Plenitude; there are here two 'voids' or two 'plenitudes' and they are mutually exclusive, just as in an hour glass the two compartments cannot be simultaneously empty or full. ~~Once it has been fully grasped that the relationship between water and drops of water parallels that between Substance and the accidents which are the contents of the world, the 'illusory' nature of these accidents cannot be a matter of doubt or present any difficulty.~~ The Islamic dictum that creatures are a proof of God means that the nature of phenomena is that of 'accidents' and that they therefore disclose the ultimate Substance. The comparison with water is imperfect in that it takes no account of the transcendence of Substance; but matter cannot offer any less inadequate picture because transcendence is always blurred in its reflections to the very degree that the plane in question partakes of accidentality.

There is discontinuity between accidents and Substance, although from Substance to accidents there is an extremely subtle continuity in the sense that, Substance alone being fully real, accidents must necessarily be aspects of it; but in that case they are being considered only in terms of their cause and not in any other terms and the irreversibility of relationship is therefore maintained. In other words the accident is then reduced to Substance; as accident it is an exteriorization of Substance and to this there corresponds the Divine Name *Ezh-Zhāhir* (The Outer). All errors concerning the world and God consist either in a 'naturalistic' denial of the discontinuity and so also of transcendence[1]—whereas it is on the basis of this transcendence

[1] It is mainly this 'scientific' prejudice, going hand in hand with a falsification and impoverishment of speculative imagination, which prevents a man like Teilhard de Chardin from conceiving the overriding discontinuity between matter and the soul, or between the natural and the supernatural orders and so leads to the evolutionary outlook, which—inverting the truth—makes everything begin with matter. A minus always presupposes an initial plus so that a seeming evolution is no more than the quite provisional unfolding of a pre-existing result; the human embryo becomes a man because that is what it

that the whole edifice of science should have been raised—or else in a failure to understand the metaphysical and 'descending' continuity which in no way abolishes the discontinuity starting from the relative. 'Brahma is not in the world' but 'all things are *Atmā*'; 'Brahma is true, the world is false' and 'He (the delivered one, the *mukta*) is Brahma'. In these statements the whole of gnosis is contained just as it is also contained in the *Shahādah* or in the two Testimonies, or in the mysteries of Christ.[1]

Now this idea is of crucial importance: metaphysical truth with all it implies lies in the very substance of intelligence: any denial or limitation of truth is always a denial or limitation of the intellect; to know the intellect is to know its consubstantial content and so the nature of things, and this is why Greek gnosis says, 'Know thyself', the Gospels say 'The Kingdom of heaven is within you', and Islam 'Who knows himself knows his Lord'.

Revelation is an objectivization of the Intellect and that is why it has the power to actualize the intelligence which has been darkened, but not abolished, by man's fall. This darkening of the intelligence may be only accidental, not fundamental and in such a case the intelligence is in principle destined for gnosis.[2] If an elementary belief cannot consciously and explicitly reach total truth that is because in its own way it also limits the intelligence and is moreover inevitably and paradoxically allied to a certain rationalism—Vishnuism shows in this respect the same phenomenon as the West—though unless

already is; no 'evolution' will produce a man from an animal embryo. In the same way the whole cosmos can only spring from an embryonic state which contains the virtuality of all its possible deployment and simply makes manifest on the plane of contingencies an infinitely higher and transcendent prototype.

[1] Trinity, Incarnation, Redemption. It is the hyperontological and gnostic Trinity which is here meant, conceived either 'vertically' (the hierarchy of the hypostases: Beyond-Being, Being, Existence; *Paramātmā, Ishwara, Buddhi*) or 'horizontally' (the intrinsic aspects or modes of the Essence: Reality, Wisdom, Bliss; *Sat, Chit, Ananda*).

[2] To say that there is a Christian gnosis means that there is a Christianity, centred on Christ as the Intellect, which defines man primarily as intelligence and not merely as fallen will or as passion. If total truth lies in the very substance of the intelligence then, for Christian gnosis, the intelligence will be the immanent Christ, 'The Light of the World'; to see in all things the divine Substance, which means to see in all things an objectivation—and in some respects a refraction—of Intelligence is to realize that 'God became man' and this without any detriment whatsoever to the literal meaning of the dogma.

there is a distortion of the faith itself it cannot become lost in this rationalism.[1] Whatever the circumstances a perspective which attributes an absolute character to relative situations, as do the exotericisms of Semitic origin, cannot be intellectually complete; but to speak of exotericism is to speak also of esotericism, and this means that the statements of the former are the symbols of the latter.

Exotericism transmits aspects or fragments of metaphysical truth (which is nothing other than the whole truth) whether about God, about the universe or about man; in man it chiefly envisages the passional and social individual; in the universe it discerns only what affects that individual; in God it hardly sees anything more than what has to do with the world—creation, man and his salvation. Consequently—and even at the risk of repetition this must be emphasized—exotericism takes no account either of pure intellect, which extends beyond the human plane and opens out on to the divine, or of pre-human and post-human cycles or of Beyond-Being, which is beyond all relativity and thus also beyond all distinctions; such a perspective is comparable to a skylight, which gives the sky a certain form, round or square maybe; through this the view of the sky is fragmentary, though certainly that does not prevent the sky from filling the room with light and life. The danger of a religious outlook based on the will is that it comes very close to insisting that faith should include a maximum of will and a minimum of intelligence; indeed intelligence is blamed, either for diminishing merit by its very nature, or for deceptively arrogating to itself both the value of merit and a knowledge such as is in reality unattainable.[2] Be that as it may it could be

[1] Cartesianism—perhaps the most intelligent way of being unintelligent—is the classi example of a faith which has become the dupe of the gropings of reasoning; this is a 'wisdom from below' and history shows it to be deadly. The whole of modern philosophy, including science, starts from a false conception of intelligence; for instance the modern cult of 'life' sins in the sense that it seeks the explanation and goal of men at a level below that of man, in something which could not serve to define the human creature; but in a much more general way all rationalism, whether direct or indirect, is false for the simple reason that it limits the intelligence to reason or intellection to logic, or in other words cause to effect.

[2] The individualism and sentimentality of a certain passional type of mysticism are undeniable facts whatever may be the spiritual virtualities of the framework taken as a whole; in this type of mysticism the intelligence has no operative function despite the possibilities of its inmost nature; an absence of metaphysical discernment brings in its train an absence of methodical concen-

Gnosticism — Pre christian and early christian beliefs — matter AS EVIL

said of religions: '~~as is the man, so for him is God~~'; in other words,
the way in which man is envisaged influences the way in which
God is envisaged and vice versa.

One point which needs to be brought out here is that ~~the criterion of metaphysical truth or of its depth lies, not in the complexity or difficulty of its expression, but in the quality and effectiveness of its symbolism~~, having regard to a particular
capacity of understanding or style of thinking.[1] Wisdom does
not lie in any complication of words but in the profundity of the
intention; assuredly the expression may according to the
circumstances be subtle and difficult, or equally it may not
be so.

At this point before going further we would digress. It is said
that a great many young people today no longer want to hear
any talk of religion or philosophy or indeed of doctrine of any
kind, that they feel everything of the kind to be outworn and
discredited and that they will respond only to what is 'concrete'
and 'lived', or even only to what is 'new'. The answer to this
mental deformation is simple enough: if the 'concrete' has
value[2] it could not be in accord with a false attitude—one which
rejects all doctrine—nor could it be wholly new; ~~there have always been religions and doctrines and this shows that their existence is in man's nature~~; for thousands of years the best of
men, men we cannot despise without making ourselves des-
picable, have promulgated and propagated doctrines and lived
according to them or died for them. The ill certainly does not
lie in the hypothetical vanity of all doctrine but solely in the

tration, the latter being the normal complement of the former. From the point
of view of gnosis the intelligence is not a part but the centre and it is the
starting point for a consciousness embracing our whole being. One thing very
characteristic of the mental climate of the traditional Occident—though it in
no way compromises true intellectuality—is the association of ideas formed
between intelligence and pride as also between beauty and sin, an association
that explains many deadly reactions which date from the Renaissance.

[1] That is why it is absurd to maintain that China produced no metaphysical
systems comparable to those of India or of the West; for this is to overlook the
fact that the yellow race is preponderantly visual and not, like the white race,
auditive and semantic, this psychic difference having nothing to do with the
level of pure intelligence.

[2] When people talk today of 'concrete facts', it is usually as if one were to
call spray 'concrete' and water 'abstract'. This is the classical confusion between accidents and substance.

fact that too many men either have not followed, or do not follow, true doctrines, or have on the contrary followed, or do follow, false doctrines; in the fact that brains have been exasperated and hearts deceived by too many inconsistent and erroneous theories; in the fact that errors beyond count,[1] errors both garrulous and pernicious, have cast discredit on truth, truth which has also to be expressed in words and is always there, even when no man pays heed to it. All too many people no longer even know what is meant by an idea, what is its value and what its function; they do not so much as suspect that perfect and definite theories have always existed, theories which are therefore on their own level fully adequate and effective, and that there is nothing to add to what has been said by the sages of old except effort on our own part to understand it. If we are human beings we cannot abstain from thought and, if we think, then we are choosing a 'doctrine'; the lassitude, the lack of imagination and the childish arrogance of disillusioned and materialistic young people changes nothing in all this. If it is modern science which has created the abnormal and deceiving conditions which afflict youth today, that is because this science is itself abnormal and deceiving. No doubt it will be said that man is not responsible for his nihilism, that it is science which has slain the gods, but this is an avowal of intellectual impotence, not a title to glory, since anyone who knows what the gods signify will not let himself be carried away by discoveries in the physical realm—which merely displace sensory symbols, but do not abolish them—and still less by gratuitous hypotheses and the errors of psychologists. Even if we know that space is an eternal night sheltering galaxies and nebulae, the sky will still stretch blue above us and symbolize the realm of angels and of Bliss.

Existence is a reality in some respects comparable to a living organism; it cannot with impunity be reduced in man's consciousness and in his modes of action to proportions that do violence to its nature; pulsations of the extra-rational[2] pass through it from every quarter. Now religion and all forms of

---

[1] 'My name is Legion', said a devil in the story of the Gadarene swine in the Gospel.

[2] Ordinarily and in every sort of context people speak of the 'irrational' but this is a dangerous abuse of terminology all too liable to reduce the supra-rational to the infra-rational.

Nihilism—traditional values senseless, all existence meaningless!

112

supra-rational wisdom belong to this non-rational order the presence of which we observe everywhere around us, unless we are blinded by a mathematician's prejudice; to attempt to treat existence as a purely arithmetical and physical reality means to falsify it in relation to ourselves and within ourselves and in the end it is to blow it to pieces.

In a germane field we must take note of the abuse of the idea of intelligence. For the present writer intelligence can have no other object than truth, just as love has beauty or goodness for its object. There can indeed be intelligence that is in error, for intelligence is mingled with contingency and by it denatured, and error, being nothing in itself, has need of the spirit; but we must never lose sight of what intelligence is in itself, nor believe that a work compounded of error could be the product of a healthy or even of a transcendent intelligence: above all cleverness and cunning must not be confused with pure intelligence and pure contemplation.[1] Intellectuality essentially includes an aspect of 'sincerity', now perfect sincerity of intelligence is inconceivable apart from disinterestedness; to know is to see and seeing is an equating of subject with object and not a passional act. 'Faith', or the acceptance of truth, should be sincere, that is to say it should be contemplative: for it is one thing to accept an idea—whether true or false—because one has some material or sentimental interest in it, quite another to accept it because one knows or believes it to be true.

Some people say that science has long since shown up the inconsistency of the Revelations, which arise—as they would argue—from our inveterate nostalgia as timid and unsatisfied earthlings:[2] in a context such as that of this book there is no

---

[1] As was pointed out in *Stations of Wisdom* (Murray 1961) in the chapter 'Orthodoxy and Intellectuality' lack of intelligence and vice may be only superficial and thus in a sense 'accidental' and remediable, just as they may also be relatively 'essential' and in practice incurable; but an essential lack of virtue is incompatible with transcendent intelligence, just as outstanding virtue is hardly ever found in a fundamentally unintelligent person. Let it be added that there are those who despise intelligence, either in the name of 'humility' or in the name of the 'concrete', while others almost regard it as a form of malice: to this St Paul has replied in anticipation (1. Cor. 14, 20): 'Brethren, be not children in understanding: howbeit in malice be ye children, but in understanding be men.'

[2] And incurably stupid earthlings, we would add, were this hypothesis true.

need to reply yet again to such a thesis, but let us nevertheless take the opportunity to add one more picture to those already given elsewhere. Imagine a radiant summer sky and imagine simple folk who gaze at it projecting into it their dream of the beyond; now suppose that it were possible to transport these simple folk into the dark and freezing abyss of the galaxies and nebulae with its overwhelming silence. In this abyss all too many of them would lose their faith, and this is precisely what happens as a result of modern science both to the learned and to the victims of popularization. What most men do not know—and if they could know it, why should they be called on to believe it?—is that this blue sky, though illusory as an optical error and belied by the vision of interplanetary space, is none the less an adequate reflection of the heaven of the angels and of the blessed and that therefore despite everything it is this blue mirage, flecked with silver clouds, which was right and will have the final say; to be astonished at this amounts to admitting that it is by chance that we are here on earth and see the sky as we do. Of course the black abyss of the galaxies also reflects something, but the symbolism is then shifted and it is no longer a question of the heaven of angels. To remain faithful to our starting point, it is no doubt in the first place a question of the terrors of the divine mysteries in which any man is lost who seeks to violate them by means of his fallible reason and without adequate motive; in a positive sense it is the *scientia sacra*, which transcends the 'faith of the simple' and is, *Deo juvante*, accessible to pure intellect:[1] but it is also a question, according to the immediate symbolism of appearances, of the abysses of universal manifestation, of this *samsāra* the limits of which indefinitely elude our ordinary experience. Finally extraterrestrial space likewise reflects death as has already been pointed out above; it is a projection outside our earthly security into a dizzy void and an unimaginable strangeness; this is something which can also be understood in a spiritual sense since, as the Prophet said, we must 'die before we die'. But what we would chiefly emphasize here is the error of believing that by the mere fact of its objective content 'science' possesses the

[1] It is precisely this *scientia sacra* which enables us to grasp that this 'faith' is right and that 'children' are not wrong when they pray turning to the blue sky, though in another fashion grace too enables us to grasp this. But nothing is possible apart from divine aid, the *tawfiq* on which Sufis insist, so that higher intelligence is not of itself a sufficient guarantee in what concerns our final goal.

~~power and the right to destroy myths and religions and that it is some kind of higher experience, which kills gods and beliefs; in reality it is human incapacity to understand unexpected phenomena or to resolve certain seeming antinomies which is smothering truth and dehumanizing the world.~~

But one further ambiguity still remains to be cleared up once for all. The word gnosis, which appears in this book and in our previous works, refers to ~~supra-rational, and thus purely intellective, knowledge of metacosmic realities.~~ Now this knowledge cannot be reduced to the 'gnosticism' of history; it would then be necessary to say that Ibn 'Arabī or Shankara were Alexandrine gnostics; in short, gnosis cannot be held responsible for every association of ideas or every abuse of terminology. It is humanly admissable not to believe in gnosis; what is quite inadmissable in anyone claiming to understand the subject is to include under this heading things having no relation of species or level with the reality in question, whatever the value attributed to that reality. In place of 'gnosis' the Arabic term *ma'rifah* or the Sanskrit term *jnāna* could just as well have been used, but a Western term seems more normal in a book written in a Western language; there is also the term 'theosophy', but this has even more unfortunate associations, while the term 'knowledge' is too general, unless its meaning is made specific by an epithet or by the context. What must be emphasized and made clear is that the term 'gnosis' is used by us in its etymological and universal sense and therefore cannot be reduced to meaning merely the Graeco-Oriental syncretism of later classical times,[1] still less can it be applied to some pseudo-religious pseudo-yogic or even merely literary fantasy.[2] If for example, Catholics can call Islam, in which they do not believe, a religion and not a pseudo-religion, there seems no reason why a similar distinction should not be made between a genuine

[1] Even though we do not reduce the meaning of this word to that syncretism we nevertheless admit for clear and historical reasons that the heretics conventionally called 'gnostics' can properly be so called. Their first fault lay in misinterpreting gnosis in dogmatical mode, thus giving rise to errors and to a sectarianism incompatible with a sapiential perspective: despite this the indirect connection with genuine gnosis can, if need be, justify the use of the term 'gnostic' in this case.

[2] As is more and more often done since psychoanalysts (in the widest sense of the term) have arrogated to themselves a monopoly in all that concerns the inner life, where they confuse together the most diverse and irreconcilable things in a common process of levelling and relativization.

gnosis having certain precise or approximate characteristics and a pseudo-gnosis devoid of them.

In order to bring out clearly that the difference between Islam and Christianity is indeed a difference of metaphysical perspective and symbolism—that these two forms of spirituality are convergent—let us attempt succinctly to characterize gnosis by starting from the key idea that Christianity means 'God became what we are, in order that we might become what He is' (St Irenaeus); Heaven became earth that earth might become Heaven. Christ re-enacts in the outer historical world what is being enacted at all times in the inner world of the soul. In man the Spirit becomes the ego in order that the ego may become pure Spirit; the Spirit or the Intellect (*Intellectus*, not *mens* or *ratio*) becomes ego by incarnating in the mind in the form of intellection, of truth, and the ego becomes the Spirit or Intellect through uniting with It.[1] Thus Christianity is a doctrine of union, or rather it is the doctrine of Union rather than of Unity: the Principle is united to manifestation so that the latter can be united to the Principle, hence the symbolism of love and the predominance of the bhaktic way. 'God became man', says St Irenaeus, 'because of the immensity of His love', and equally man must unite himself with God through 'love', whatever meaning—volitive, emotional or intellectual—be given to that term. 'God is Love': as the Trinity He is Union and He wishes union.

Now what is the content of the Spirit; in other words, what is Christ's sapiential message? For that which is this message is also, in our microcosm, the eternal content of the Intellect. This message or content is: love God with all your faculties and, in function of this love, love your neighbour as yourself; that is, become united—for in essence to 'love' means to become united —with the Heart-Intellect and, in function or as a condition of

[1] 'The Spirit penetrates all things, yea the deep things of God. For what man knoweth the things of a man, save the spirit of man which is in him? even so the things of God knoweth no man, but the Spirit of God. Now we have received, not the spirit of the world, but the spirit which is of God; that we might know the things that are freely given to us of God.' (1. Cor. II, 10-12.) For Dante the damned are those who have lost the good of the Intellect (*Inferno*, III, 18) and this can be related to the microcosmic and human reflection of the Divine Intellect as well as to that Intellect Itself.

this union, abandon all pride and all passion and discern the Spirit in every creature. 'What ye shall have done unto the least of these my little ones ye shall have done it unto Me.' The Heart-Intellect, the Christ in us, is not only light or discernment but also warmth and bliss and thus 'love'; the 'light' becomes 'warm' to the degree that it becomes our being.[1]

This message—or innate truth—of the Spirit prefigures the cross since there are here two dimensions, one 'vertical' and the other 'horizontal'; namely love of God and love of the neighbour, or union with the Spirit and union with the human setting, this latter being envisaged as a manifestation of the Spirit or as the 'mystical body'. From a slightly different point of view these two dimensions are represented respectively by knowledge and love: man 'knows' God and 'loves' his neighbour, or again man loves God most through knowing Him and knows his neighbour best by loving him. As for the grievous aspect of the cross it must be said that from the point of view of gnosis more than from any other, both in ourselves and among men, it is profoundly true that 'the light shineth in darkness; and the darkness comprehended it not'.[2]

The whole of Christianity is expressed in the doctrine of the Trinity and fundamentally this doctrine represents a perspective of union; it sees union already *in divinis*: God prefigures in His very nature the relationship between Himself and the world, these relationships becoming 'external' only in an illusory mode.

As has been pointed out already the Christian religion lays stress on the 'phenomenal' content of faith rather than on its intrinsic and transforming quality; we say 'lays stress' and 'rather than' to show there is here no unconditional definition; the Trinity does not belong to the phenomenal order, but it is none the less a function of the phenomenon of Christ. In so far

[1] That is why the 'love' (*mahabbah*) of the Sufis, does not at all presuppose a bhaktic way, any more than the use by Shaiva Vedantists of the term *bhakti* implies any Vaishnava dualism in their outlook.

[2] The gnostic dimension—and again this is to be taken in its etymological and timeless meaning—stands out in the clearest possible way in a passage in the recently discovered Gospel of Thomas which relates how Christ, after speaking to the Apostles, went out with St Thomas and spoke three words or sentences to him. When Thomas returned alone the other disciples pressed him with questions, and he said that were he to confide to them even one of these sayings they would stone him and that fire would then leap forth from the stones to devour them.

as the object of faith is 'principial' it coincides with the intellectual or contemplative nature of faith[1] but in so far as its content is 'phenomenal' faith will be 'volitive'. Broadly speaking Christianity is an 'existential' way,[2] though 'intellectualized' in gnosis, whereas Islam is on the contrary an 'intellectual' way 'phenomenalized', which means that it is *a priori* intellectual, either directly or indirectly according to whether we are speaking of the *haqīqah* or of the *sharī'ah*; the Moslem, firm in his unitary conviction, which certitude at bottom coincides with the very substance of intelligence and thus with the Absolute,[3] readily sees in phenomena temptations to 'associations' (*shirk, mushrik*) whereas the Christian, centred as he is on the fact of Christ and on the miracles flowing in essence from that fact, feels an inherent distrust of intelligence—which he is apt to take to be the equivalent of 'wisdom after the flesh' in contrast to the Pauline charity (*agape*)—and of what he believes to be the pretensions of the human spirit.

Now if, from the point of view of realization or of the Way, Christianity operates through love of God—a love which responds to the divine love for man, God being Himself Love—Islam as we have already seen proceeds through 'sincerity in unitary faith' and we know this faith must imply all the consequences logically following from its content—which is Unity, or the Absolute. First there is *el-imān*, the accepting of Unity by man's intelligence; then, since we exist both individually and collectively, there is *el-islām*, the submission of man's will to Unity, or to the idea of Unity, this second element relating to Unity considered as a synthesis on the plane of multiplicity; and finally there is *el-ihsān*, which expands or deepens the two previous elements to the point of their ultimate consequence. Under the influence of *el-ihsān*, *el-imān* becomes 'realization' or 'a certitude that is lived'—'knowing' becoming 'being'—while *el-islām*, instead of being limited to a certain number of pre-

[1] This is what is meant by the Islamic saying that at birth the soul is Moslem—or Christian, according to the religion—but that it is men who turn it away from its innate faith or on the contrary 'confirm' that faith. This recalls the 'recollection' of Plato.

[2] Being, since it is founded on the element *Sat*, 'Being', of the Vedantic terminology and not directly on the element *Chit*, 'Consciousness', although the Logos intrinsically relates to the latter element, and this opens up the dimension of gnosis. The Intellect became phenomenal in order that the phenomenal might become Intellect.

[3] But it goes without saying that this definition is applicable to all gnosis.

scribed attitudes, comes to include every level in man's nature; in the beginning faith and submission are hardly more than symbolical attitudes, although none the less efficacious at their own level. By virtue of *el-ihsān*, *imān* becomes gnosis, or participation in the divine Intelligence, and *islām* becomes 'extinction' in the divine Being; since participation in the divine is a mystery no man has a right to proclaim himself a *mu'min* ('believing', one possessing *imān*) though he can perfectly well call himself *muslim* ('submitted', one conforming to *Islām*); *imān* is a secret between the servant and his Lord like the *ihsān* which determines its level, or 'station' (*maqām*), or 'secret' (*sirr*), its ineffable reality. In unitary faith—with the fullness of its consequences—as in total love of God, it is a question of escaping from the dispersing and mortal multiplicity of all that which —being 'other than He'—is not, a question of escaping from sin because sin implies a love that is in practice total for the creature or the created, a love turned aside therefore from God-who-is-Love and squandered into fragments on what is inferior to man's immortal personality. Here we find a criterion that clearly shows the meaning of religions and modes of Wisdom: it is 'concentration' in function of truth and with a view to rediscovering, beyond death and this world of death, all we loved here below; but all this is for us hidden in a geometrical point, which at the outset appears to us like an utter impoverishment and indeed is so in a certain relative sense and in relation to our world of deceptive richness, of sterile segmentation into a myriad of facets or refractions. The world is a movement which already bears within itself the principle of its own exhaustion, a deployment which displays at every point the stigmata of its narrowness and in which Life and the Spirit are astray, not by some absurd chance but because this encounter between inert Existence and living Consciousness is a possibility and thus something which cannot not be, something posited by the very infinitude of the Absolute.

At this point something must be said about the priority of contemplation. As we know Islam defines this supreme function of man in the *hadīth* about *ihsān* which calls on a man to 'adore Allah as though thou didst see Him' since 'if thou dost not see Him, He none the less sees thee'; Christianity from its angle calls first for total love of God and only after this for love of the neighbour; now it must be insisted in the interest of the love of God that this second love could not be total because love of ourselves is not so; whether *ego* or *alter*, man is not God.[1] In any case it follows from all traditional definitions of man's supreme function that a man capable of contemplation has no right to neglect it but is on the contrary 'called' to dedicate himself to it; in other words he sins neither against God nor against his neighbour—to say the very least—in following the example of Mary in the Gospels and not that of Martha, for contemplation contains action and not the reverse. If in point of fact action can be opposed to contemplation it is nevertheless not opposed to it in principle, nor is action called for beyond what is necessary or required by the duties of a man's station in life. In abasing ourselves from humility we must not also abase things which transcend us, for then our virtue loses all its value and meaning; to reduce spirituality to a 'humble' utilitarianism—that is, to a mild kind of materialism—is to cast aspersions on God, on the one hand because it is like saying it is not worth while to be over-preoccupied with God and on the other hand because it means relegating the divine gift of intelligence to the rank of the superfluous.

Apart from this, and on a vaster scale, it must be understood that a 'metaphysical point of view' is synonymous with 'inwardness': metaphysic is not 'external' to any form of spirituality, it is thus impossible to consider something both metaphysically and from the outside at one and the same time; furthermore, those who uphold the extra-intellectual principle according to which any possible competence would derive exclusively from a practical participation do not refrain from laying down the law 'intellectually' and in full awareness of what they are doing,[2] about forms of spirituality in which they do not participate in any way whatever.

Intelligence can be the essence of a Way provided there is a contemplative mentality and a thinking that is fundamentally non-passional; an exotericism could not, as such, constitute

[1] As for the *hadīth* just cited it does not keep silent on human charity since, before defining *ihsān*, it defines *islām* and this consists *inter alia* in the paying of the tithe or *zakāh*.

[2] For example by pretending that the Absolute of the Vedanta or of Sufism is only a 'natural' absolute, 'devoid of life' and therefore 'a deception', and so on.

ASPERSIONS — Defamations

this way but can, as in the case of Islam, predispose to it by its fundamental perspective, its structure and its 'climate'. ~~From the strictly *sharaite* point of view intelligence is reduced, for Islam, to responsibility; viewed thus every responsible person is intelligent~~; in other words a 'responsible person' is defined in relation to intelligence and not merely in relation to freedom of the will.[1]

At the beginning of this book we saw that Islam is founded on the nature of things in the sense that it sees ~~the condition for salvation in our theomorphism, that is to say, in the total character of human intelligence, in free will and in the gift of speech, provided these faculties are respectively—thanks to an 'objective' divine intervention—~~vehicles for certitude, for moral equilibrium and for unitive prayer; we have further seen that these three modes of theomorphism and their contents are, broadly speaking, represented in the Islamic tradition by the triad *Imān—Islām—Ihsān* (Faith—Law—Way). Now to speak of something as theomorphic is to refer to characteristics proper to the divine nature, and in fact God is 'Light' (*Nūr*),[2] 'Life' (*Hayāt*) or 'Will' (*Irādah*) and 'Word' (*Kalām, Kalimah*); this Word is the creative word *Kun* (Be!);[3] but what is, with God, creative power is, with man, transmuting and deifying power; if the divine Word creates, the human word responding to it— the 'mentioning' of Allah—brings back to God. The divine Word first creates, then reveals; the human word first transmits, then transforms; it transmits the truth and then, addressing itself to God, transforms and deifies man; human transmission corresponds to divine Revelation and deification to Creation. ~~Speech in man has no right function but to transmit truth and deification; it is either true discourse or else prayer.~~[4]

[1] 'They will say: Had we but listened or had we but understood (*na'qilu* with intelligence: *'aql*) we would not be among the guests of the furnace.' (Quran LXVII, 10.) Islamic evaluation of the intelligence is also revealed in this *hadīth* among others: 'our Lord Jesus said: It was not impossible for me to raise the dead, but it was impossible for me to cure the stupid'.

[2] Infinite 'Consciousness' free from all objectivation.

[3] Hence the word *kawn*, the 'world', 'that which exists'. *El-kawn el-kabīr* is the macrocosm: *el-kawn eş-şaghīr*, the microcosm.

[4] 'But let your communication be, Yea, yea; Nay, nay: for whatsoever is more than these cometh of evil' (Matt. V, 37). This is akin to the 'sincerity' (*ikhlāş*) which is the very essence of *Ihsān* according to the following traditional

Let us here briefly sum up the whole of this doctrine: in order to be able to understand the meaning of the Quran as a sacrament one must know that it is the uncreated prototype of the gift of speech, that it is the eternal Word of God (*kalāmu 'Llāh*) and that man and God meet in the revealed speech, in the Logos which has taken on the differentiated form of human language in order that, through this language, man may find again the undifferentiated and saving Word of the Eternal. All this explains the immense saving power of the 'theophoric' word, its capacity to convey a divine power and to annihilate a legion of sins.[1]

The second foundation of the Way, as was pointed out at the beginning of this chapter, is contemplative or operative concentration, or prayer in all its forms and at all levels. The support of this concentration—or of quintessential prayer—is in Islam 'mentioning' or 'remembrance' (*dhikr*)[2] a term the meaning of which ranges from the recitation of the whole of the Quran to the mystical exhalation which symbolizes the final *hā* of the Name *Allāh* or the initial *hā* of the Name *Hua*, 'He'. Everything that can be said of the divine Name—for example, that 'all things on earth are accursed save the remembrance of Allah', or that 'nothing makes the wrath of Allah so distant as this remembrance'—all this can equally be said of the heart and of the intellect[3] and, by extension, of metaphysical intellection and contemplative concentration. In the heart we are united to

definition: 'Virtue in action (spiritual actualization, *el-ihsān*) is to adore God as if thou didst see Him, and, if thou seest Him not, none the less He sees thee.' Truthful speech is the very symbol of that right intent which in Islam is everything. 'Lead us on the straight path' (*eṣ-ṣirāt el-mustaqīm*), says the *Fātihah*.

[1] 'And Adam received words from his Lord' (Quran, I, 38). In a certain trinitarian theology the 'Word' represents the 'Knowledge' which 'Being' has of Itself. 'For my Father is greater than I' (John, XIV, 28): 'Being' is in itself greater than the pole of 'Consciousness', although each of these is in reality Being, in its intrinsic nature. Moreover Being also has an aspect of 'Consciousness' in relation to Beyond-Being in the sense that It crystallizes the potentialities of Beyond-Being distinctively with a view to their manifestation; but Beyond-Being is none the less the supreme 'Self', whose infinite Knowledge is undifferentiated by reason of Its very infinity.

[2] 'He who mentions Me in himself (*fī nafsihi*), I will mention him in Myself, and he who mentions Me in an assembly, him I will mention in an assembly better than his' (*Hadīth qudsī*). The 'better' assembly is that of heaven. According to another *hadīth* belonging to the same category: 'I hold company (*Innī jālis*) with him who mentions Me.'

[3] 'Heaven and earth cannot contain Me, but the heart of My believing servant does contain Me' (*Hadīth qudsī*).

pure Being and in the intellect to total Truth, these two being coincident in the Absolute.[1]

In Islam concentration appears as 'sincerity' in prayer; prayer is fully valid only on condition of being sincere and it is this sincerity—and so in fact this concentration—which 'opens' the *dhikr*, or enables it to be simple while at the same time having an immense effect.[2] To the objection that jaculatory prayer is an easy and external thing, that it could neither efface a thousand sins nor have the value of a thousand good works, the tradition answers that from the human side the whole merit lies, first in the intention that makes us pronounce the prayer— apart from the intention we would not pronounce it—and secondly in our recollectedness, and thus in our 'presence' in face of the Presence of God; but that this human merit is as nothing in the eyes of grace.

The 'remembrance of God' is at the same time a forgetting of self; conversely, the ego is a kind of crystallization of forget- fulness of God. The brain is, as it were, the organ of this forget- fulness;[3] it is like a sponge filled with pictures of this world of dispersion and heaviness, filled too with the tendencies of the ego towards both dispersal and hardening. As for the heart, it is the latent remembrance of God, hidden deep down in our 'I', in prayer it is as if the heart, risen to the surface, came to take the place of the brain which then sleeps with a holy slumber; this slumber unites and soothes and its most elementary trace in the soul is peace. 'I sleep, but my heart waketh.'[4]

If Ibn Arabī and others require—in conformity with the Quran and the Sunna—that a man should 'become penetrated by the majesty of Allah' before and during the practice of *dhikr*, they imply, not merely a reverential attitude rooted in

[1] 'Oh, happy man' sings Jāmī, 'whose heart has been illumined by invoca- tion (*dhikr*), in the shade of which the carnal soul has been vanquished, the thought of multiplicity chased away, the invoker (*dhākir*) transmuted into invocation and the invocation transmuted into the Invoked (*madhkūr*).'

[2] To the 'effort of actualization' (*istihdār*) of the servant there answers the 'presence' (*hudūr*) of the Lord.

[3] Fallen man is by definition 'forgetfulness'; consequently the Way is 'remembrance'. An Arabic proverb, based on the phonetic connection between the words *nasiya* ('to forget') and *insān* ('man'), says that the first forgetful being (*awwalu nāsin*) was the first man (*awwalu 'nnās*).

[4] The Prophet said: 'Protect God in thine heart; then God shall protect thee.'

the imagination and in feeling, but a conformity of man's whole being to the 'Motionless Mover', which in brief means a return to our normative archetype, to the pure 'Adamic' substance 'made in the image of God', and this is moreover directly connected with dignity, the role of which is clearly to be seen in the sacerdotal and royal functions: priest and king both stand before the divine Being, over the people, and it might be said that they are at the same time 'something of God'. In a certain sense ~~the dignity of the *dhākir*—of him who prays—connects with the 'image' Divinity takes on in relation to him~~, or in other words this dignity—this 'holy silence' or this 'non-action'—is the very image of the divine Principle. Buddhism gives us a particularly concrete example of this: the sacramental image of the Buddha is at the same time 'divine form' and human perfection and marks the meeting point between the earthly and the heavenly. But all this refers to contemplative prayer alone and it is precisely this prayer which is in question where the sufic *dhikr* is concerned.

The Name Allāh, which is the quintessence of all the Quranic formulas, consists of two syllables linked by the double *lam*; this *lam* is like the bodily death which precedes the beyond and the resurrection, or like the spiritual death which inaugurates illumination and sanctity, and this analogy is capable of being extended to the universe, either in an ontological or in a cyclical sense: between two degrees of reality, whether envisaged in relation to their concatenation or, should such be the case, their succession, there is always a kind of extinction[1] and this is what is also expressed by the word *illā* ('if it be not') in the *Shahādah*.[2] ~~The first syllable of the Name refers, according to a self-evident interpretation, to the world and to life inasmuch as they are divine manifestations, and the second to God and to the beyond or to immortality.~~ While the Name begins with a sort of hiatus between silence and utterance (the *hamzah*) like a *creatio ex nihilo*, it ends in an unlimited expulsion of breath which symbolically opens into the Infinite—that is, the final *hā* marks

---

[1] In the canonical prayer of Islam, which includes phases of abasement and rising up—or more exactly of bowing down and straightening up again followed by prostration and rest—the former are related to death or 'extinction' and the latter to resurrection or immortality, 'permanence'; the passage from one phase to the other is marked by the pronouncing of the *takbīr*: 'God is greater' (*Allāhu akbar*).

[2] This is the 'strait' or 'narrow' gate of the Gospels.

the supra-ontological Non-Duality[1]—and this indicates that there is no symmetry between the initial nothingness of things and the transcendent Non-Being. Thus the Name Allah embraces all that 'is'[2] from the Absolute down to the tiniest grain of dust whereas the Name *Hua*, 'He', which 'personifies' the final *hā*, indicates the Absolute as such in Its ineffable transcendence and Its inviolable mystery.

There is of necessity a guarantee of efficacy in the divine Names themselves. In Amida Buddhism[3] the saving certitude of the practice of invocation is derived from the 'original vow' of Amida but fundamentally this amounts to saying that in every analogous practice in other traditional forms this certitude is derived from the very meaning included in the *mantram* or divine Name. Thus, if the *Shahādah* includes the same grace as the 'original vow' of Amida,[4] it is by virtue of its very content: because it is the supreme formulation of Truth and because Truth delivers by its very nature. To identify oneself with Truth, to infuse It into our being and to transfer our being into it is to escape from the empire of error and malice. Now the *Shahādah* is nothing other than an exteriorization in doctrinal form of the Name Allah; it corresponds strictly to the *Ehieh asher Ehieh* of the Burning Bush in the Torah; it is by such formulas that God announces 'Who He is', and so what His Name signifies; and it is for this reason that such formulas, or such *mantrams*, are so many Names of God.[5]

We have just pointed out that the meaning of the Name Allah is that *lā ilahā illa Llāh*; that cosmic manifestation is illusory and the metacosmic Principle alone is real. In order to make our meaning more clear we must here repeat a *haqīqah* already touched on in the chapter on the Quran; since from the

---

[1] This is what is expressed by the formula: 'Allah is neither Himself nor other than Himself' (*Allāhu lā hua wa lā ghairuhu*). This proposition is equally applicable in a different sense to the qualities (*ṣīfat*) of God.

[2] *El-ulūhiyah*—'Allahness'—is indeed defined as the 'sum of the mysteries of Reality' (*jumlatu haqā'iq al-Wujūd*).

[3] This term, derived from the Japanese, is used because in the West it designates conventionally a Buddhism based on incantation, one which was Chinese before becoming Japanese and Indian before becoming Chinese. Nevertheless it was in Japan that it came to its extraordinary flowering.

[4] We could say as much of the Names of Jesus and Mary and of the jaculatory prayers containing these Names.

[5] The *Shahādah* is in fact deemed to be a 'Divine Name'.

point of view of manifestation—which is our point of view, seeing that we exist—the world does indisputably have a certain reality, it must follow that the truth concerning it in a positive sense is also included in the first *Shahādah*; in fact it is so included in the form of the second *Shahādah—Muhammadun Rasūlu 'Llāh*—which springs from the word *illā* (if not) in the first *Shahādah* and means that ~~manifestation does have a relative reality which reflects the Principle~~. This testimony opposes to the total negation of transitory things—or of 'accidents'—a relative affirmation, an affirmation of manifestation inasmuch as it reflects the divine, in other words of the world as divine manifestation. *Muhammad* is the world envisaged in respect of perfection; *Rasūl* indicates the relationship of causality and thus connects the world to God. When the intellect is placed at the level of absolute Reality the relative truth is as it were absorbed by the total truth: from the point of view of verbal symbols it then finds itself as it were withdrawn into the metaphysical 'conditional' which is the word *illā*. As there is nothing outside Allah the world too must be comprised in Him and cannot be 'other than He' (*ghairuhu*): and that is why manifestation 'is the Principle' inasmuch as the Principle is 'The Outward' (*Ezh-Zhāhir*), the Principle as such being 'The Inward' (*El-Bātin*). Thus it is that the Name Allah includes all that is and surpasses all that is.[1]

In order to make quite clear the position of the formula of consecration (the *Basmalah*) in all these relationships let us add this: just as the second *Shahādah* springs from the first—from the word *illā* which is both the ontological 'isthmus' and the axis of the world—so the *Basmalah* springs from the double

---

[1] 'I persevered in this exercise till it was revealed to me:"God has said of Himself that He is the First (*El-Awwal*) and the Last (*El-Akhir*), the Inner (*El-Bātin*) and the Outer (*Ezh-Zhāhir*)." I fought against this, concentrating on my exercise, but the more I made efforts to thrust it away the more it assailed me without respite. At length I answered: "I understand that God is the First and the Last and the Inner, but that he is equally the Outward I do not understand, since outwardly I see only the universe." I received this reply: "If the term 'the Outward' were used to denote other than what thou seest then (it would be a misuse of words for) the reference would be to what is inward and not to what is outward; but I tell you that He is the Outward." At that very instant I suddenly realized the truth that there is no existence outside God and that the universe is nothing save He. . . .' (*The Rasā'il* of Shaikh Mulay El-Arabī Ed-Darqāwī).

lam in the middle of the word *Allāh*;[1] but whereas the second
Shahādah (the Testimony as to the Prophet) marks an ascending
and liberating movement, the *Basmalah* indicates a descent that
is creative, revealing and merciful, in effect it starts with
Allāh (*bismi 'Llāhi*) and ends with *Rahīm* whereas the second
Shahādah starts with *Muhammad* and ends with *Allah* (*rasūlu
'Llah*). The first *Shahādah*—with the second which it bears
within itself—is as it were the content or message of the
Basmalah; but it is also its principle, for the supreme Name
'means' the *Shahādah* once it is envisaged in a distinctive or
discursive mode; in this case it can be said that the *Basmalah*
arises from the divine *illā*. The *Basmalah* is distinguished from
the *Shahādah* by the fact that it marks a 'coming forth' as is
indicated by the words 'in the Name of' (*bismi*), whereas the
Shahādah is, either the divine 'content' or the 'message': it is
either the sun or the image of the sun, but not the sun's ray,
although from another point of view it can also be conceived
as a 'ladder' linking cosmic 'nothingness' to pure Reality.

In the *hadīth*: 'He who invokes God to the point when his
eyes overflow from fear and the earth is watered by his tears,
him God will not punish on the Day of the Resurrection', it
is not solely a question of the gift of tears or of *bhakti*, but above
all of the 'liquefying' of our post-edenic hardness, a fusion or
dissolving of which tears—or sometimes melting snow—are
traditionally the symbol. But nothing forbids us to pursue the
chain of key images; we may, for instance, pause at the symbolism of the eyes and note that the right eye corresponds to the
sun, to activity, to the future, and the left eye to the moon, to
the past, to passivity: we have here two dimensions of the ego,
the one relating to the future inasmuch as it is the leaven of
illusion and the other to the past inasmuch as it is an accumu-
lation of ego-forming experiences; in other words both the past
and the future of the ego—what we are and what we want to

[1] The four words of the Basmalah (*Bismi 'Llāhi 'Rrahmāni 'Rrahīm*) are
represented as four streams of Paradise springing forth beneath the throne of
God, which is *Er-Rūh*. The *lam* in the supreme Name and the *illā* in the Testimony correspond to the 'throne' in the sense that they 'inaugurate' the former
the syllable *Lāh* and the latter the Name *Allāh* and so 'the dimensions of
transcendence'. This follows from the nature of things and is pointed out in
order to show, in connection with practices of incantation and sapiential
doctrines, how the basic enunciations or symbols serve as vehicles for the whole
Divine Message, somewhat as a crystal synthesises the whole of space.

become or to possess—must be 'dissolved' in a present filled with a lightning flash of transpersonal contemplation, whence the 'fear' (*khashyah*) mentioned in the *hadīth* quoted above. 'His eyes overflow' (*fādhat 'aynāhu*) and 'the earth is watered' (*yuṣību 'l-ardh*): there is both an inner and an outward lique-faction and the latter corresponds to the former; when the ego is 'liquefied' the outer world, from which it is in large measure compounded, seems to be drawn into the same alchemical process in the sense that it becomes 'transparent' so that the contemplative sees God everywhere, or sees all things in God.

Let us now consider prayer in its most general sense: the call to God, if it is to be perfect or 'sincere', must be fervent, just as concentration, if it is to be perfect must be pure; now at the level of emotive piety the key to concentration is fervour. ~~The answer to the question of knowing how one escapes from luke-warmness and realizes fervour or concentration is that zeal depends on our awareness of our goal;~~ a man who is indifferent or lazy knows well enough how to hurry when threatened by danger or when enticed by something agreeable[1] and this is as much as to say that zeal may be motivated either by fear or by love. ~~But equally, and *a fortiori*, its motive may be knowledge,~~ knowledge too—to the degree that it is real—supplies us with sufficient reasons for ardour, otherwise it would be necessary to hold that man—every man—is only capable of action when under the impulsion of threats or promises; this is certainly true of collectivities but it is not true of every individual.

The very fact of our existence is a prayer and compels us to prayer so that it could indeed be said: 'I am, therefore I pray; *sum ergo oro*'. Existence is by nature ambiguous and from this it follows that it compels us to prayer in two ways: first by its quality of being a divine expression, a coagulated and seg-

---

[1] 'Blessed are they that have not seen and yet have believed', says the Gospel and we find the same idea in the *hadīth* about *ihsān*: '. . . And if thou dost not see him (God), none the less He seeth thee.' Gnosis, far from seeking to abolish these teachings, situates them somewhat differently, for there is not only the difference between earthly ignorance—which requires 'faith'—and heavenly knowledge, but also the difference between doctrinal learning and unitive realization: such learning is by no means 'blind' in itself, but it is so in relation to realization 'in depth'.

mented mystery, and, secondly, by its inverse aspect of being a bondage and perdition, so that we must indeed 'think of God' not merely because, being men, we cannot not take account of the divine basis of existence—in so far as we are faithful to our nature—but also because we are by the same token forced to recognize that we are fundamentally more than existence and that we live like exiles in a house on fire.[1] ~~On the one hand existence is a surge of creative joy and every creature praises God; to exist is to praise God whether we be waterfalls, trees, birds or men; but on the other hand existence means not to be God and so to be in a certain respect ineluctably in opposition to Him;~~ existence is something which grips us like a shirt of Nessus. Someone who does not know the house is on fire has no reason to call for help, just as the man who does not know he is drowning will not clutch the rope that could save him; but ~~to know we are perishing means, either to despair or else to pray.~~ Truly to know that we are nothing because the whole world is nothing, means to remember 'That which Is'[2] and through this remembrance to become free. If a man has a nightmare and then, while still dreaming starts calling on God for aid, he infallibly awakens; this shows two things: first, that conscious intelligence of the Absolute subsists in sleep as a distinct personality—our spirit remaining apart from our states of illusion—and secondly that when a man calls on God he will end by awakening also from that great dream which is life, the world, the ego. If this call can breach the wall of common

[1] Like existence fire is something two-faced, for it is both light and heat, divinity and hell. In *The Language of the Self* (Ganesh, 1959) we made incidental reference to a Hindu theory in which fire, inasmuch as it has a tendency to rise and to illumine, corresponds to *sattwa*, whereas water, inasmuch as it spreads out horizontally and fertilizes, is assimilable to *rajas*, while earth then relates to *tamas* through its inertia and its crushing force; but it goes without saying that in another respect fire relates to *rajas* through its devouring and 'passionate' heat, light alone then corresponding to *sattwa*; in this case we have the triad not of the visible elements—fire, water and earth—but of the sensory functions of 'fire-sun': luminosity, heat and, negatively, darkness. Pure luminosity is cold through its transcendence; darkness is so through privation. Spiritually speaking darkness freezes whereas light refreshes.

[2] In expressions such as this we are not taking account of the limitation of 'Being': this word is being used in an extrinsic sense in relation to the world and without in any way prejudicing the intrinsic limitlessness of the Divine. Theology does exactly the same as also does Sufism, which does not hesitate to speak of the existence (*wujūd*) of Allah; it is the intention—clear for the gnostic—and not the literal meaning of the term which settles the required sense.

dreams, why should it not also breach the wall of that vaster and more tenacious dream-existence?

~~There is, in this call, no egoism, for pure prayer is the most intimate and most precious form of the gift of self.~~[1] The common man is in the world to receive and, even if he gives alms, he steals from God—and robs himself—in so far as he supposes that his gift is all that God and his neighbour can ask of him; letting 'his left hand know what his right hand doeth' he always expects either consciously or unconsciously something from his surroundings. It is necessary to acquire the habit of the inner gift apart from which all alms are but half-gifts; and what one gives to God is by that very fact given to all men.

If we start from the idea that intellection and concentration, or doctrine and method, are the foundations of the way, it should be added that these two elements are valid and effective only by virtue of a traditional guarantee, a 'seal' coming from Heaven. ~~Intellection has need of tradition, of a Revelation fixed in time and adapted to a society,~~ if it is to be awakened in us and not go astray, and prayer identifies itself with the Revelation or proceeds from it as we have already seen; in other words the importance of orthodoxy, of tradition, of Revelation is that the means of realizing the Absolute must come 'objectively' from the Absolute; ~~knowledge cannot spring up 'subjectively' except within the framework of an 'objective' divine formulation of Knowledge.~~

But this element of 'tradition', precisely because of its impersonal and formal character, requires a complement which is essentially personal and free, and this complement is virtue: without virtue orthodoxy becomes pharisaical, in a subjective sense of course for its objective incorruptibility is not in question.

If we have defined metaphysic as discernment between the Real and the unreal, then virtue will be defined as the inversion of the relationship between *ego* and *alter*, this relationship being a natural, though illusory inversion of the real 'proportions', and so a 'fall' and a rupture of equilibrium (for the fact that two

[1] A *hadīth* says: 'The last hour shall not come until there is no longer any man on earth who says: *Allāh! Allāh!*' Indeed it is sanctity and wisdom—and along with these universal and quintessential prayer—which sustain the world.

people believe themselves to be 'I' proves that, on pain of absurdity, neither is right, the 'I' being logically unique) virtue is the inversion and so the rectifying of that fall; in a way that is effective although relative virtue sees the 'I' in 'the other' or the converse. This brings out clearly the sapiential function of virtue: charity, far from being reducible to sentimentality or utilitarianism, effectuates a state of consciousness, it aims at the real, not at the illusory; it confers a sight of reality on our personal 'being', on our volitive nature, and is not limited to a mode of thought involving no obligation. In the same way we can say of humility that when properly conceived it realizes in us consciousness of our own nothingness in face of the Absolute and of our imperfection by comparison with other men; like every virtue it is at the same time cause and effect. Like spiritual exercises, though in a different way, the virtues are fixing agents for what is known by the spirit.[1]

There is an error which all too easily arises in the minds of those who turn to metaphysics in a reaction against a conventional religiosity, the error of believing that truth has no need of God, of the personal God who both sees and hears us, nor of our virtues either; that it has nothing to do with what is human and that consequently it is enough for us to know that the Principle is not manifestation and so forth, just as though these ideas gave us a dispensation from being men and—to put it at the very lowest—immunized us against the rigours of natural laws. Had destiny not so willed—and destiny does not depend on our ideas about doctrine—we should have no knowledge nor even any life; God is in all that we are and He alone can give us life and light and protection. In the same way as regards the virtues: assuredly the truth has no need of our personal qualities and may even lie beyond our destinies, but we have need of truth and must bow to its requirements, which do not concern only the mind;[2] since we exist, our

---

[1] The sentimentality with which people surround the virtues leads to their being easily falsified; for many people humility means despising an intelligence they have not got. The devil has got hold of charity and made of it a demagogic or Godless utilitarianism and an argument against contemplation, as though Christ had supported Martha against Mary. Humility becomes servility and charity materialism; in practice this kind of virtue seeks to furnish the proof that one can get along without God.

[2] 'When a man talks of God without having true virtue,' says Plotinus, 'his words are but hollow.' He is referring, not to simple enunciations that are in accord with orthodoxy, but to spontaneous utterances deemed to spring from a direct knowledge.

being—whatever the content of our mind—must at every level be in accord with its divine principle. The cataphatic, and thus in some degree 'individualistic', virtues are the keys to the apophatic virtues, and these latter are inseparable from gnosis. The virtues testify to the beauty of God. It is illogical and pernicious—both for oneself and for others—to think the truth and to forget generosity.

Here is may be convenient to explain that those virtues are termed by us 'apophatic' which are not the 'productions' of man but on the contrary radiate from the nature of Being: in relation to us they are pre-existent so that the part played by us in relation to them is that of removing everything in ourselves which opposes their radiation and not that of producing them 'positively'; here lies the whole difference between individual effort and purifying knowledge. It is in any case absurd to believe that the Sufi who states that he has gone beyond some particular virtue, or even all virtues, is on that account deprived of the qualities which go to make man's nobility and apart from which there can be no sanctity; the sole difference is that he no longer 'lives' these qualities as 'his own' and so has no feeling of any 'personal' merit as is the case with the ordinary virtues.[1] It is a matter of a divergence of principle or of nature, although from another more general and less 'operative' point of view every virtue or even every cosmic quality can be envisaged apophatically, that is, according to the ontological essence of phenomena; this is what devout people express after their own fashion when they attribute their virtues wholly to the grace of God.

In conformity with the injunctions of the Quran 'remembrance of God' requires the fundamental virtues and, arising from them, the acts of virtue called for by particular circumstances. Now the fundamental and universal virtues, inseparable from human nature, are these: humility or self-effacement, charity or generosity, truthfulness or sincerity and so impartiality; next come watchfulness or perseverance, contentment or patience.

---

[1] In his *Hikam* Ibn 'Atā-Illāh says: 'If you could only attain to Him after eliminating all your blemishes and extinguishing your egoism, you would never attain to Him. But if He wishes to lead you to Him He covers over your qualities with His qualities and your characteristics with His characteristics and unites you to Himself by virtue of what comes back to you from Him and not because of what comes back to Him from you'.

~~and lastly that~~ 'quality of being' which constitutes unitive
piety, spiritual plasticity, a disposition to saintliness.[1]

All that has been said up to this point makes possible an
explanation of the meaning of the virtues and of moral laws;
the latter are styles of action conforming to particular spiritual
perspectives and particular material and mental conditions,
while the virtues on the contrary represent intrinsic beauties
fitted into these styles and finding through them their realization. ~~Every virtue and every morality is a mode of equilibrium,
or, to be more precise, it is a way of participating, even to the
detriment of some external and false equilibrium, in the universal
Equilibrium;~~ by remaining at the centre a man escapes from
the vicissitudes of the moving periphery; and this is the meaning
of the Taoist 'non-action'. Morality is a way of acting, whereas
virtue is a way of being—a way of being wholly oneself, beyond
the ego, or of being simply that which is.[2] This could also be
expressed as follows; the various moralities are at the same time
frameworks for the virtues and their application to collectivities;
the virtue of the collectivity is its equilibrium determined by
Heaven. Moralities are diverse, but virtue, as it has been here
defined, is everywhere the same, for everywhere man is man.
~~This moral unity of humankind goes hand in hand with its
intellectual unity: perspectives and dogmas differ but truth is
one.~~

Another fundamental element of the way is symbolism,
which is manifested both in sacred art and in virgin nature.
No doubt sensory forms do not possess the same importance as
verbal or scriptural symbols, but none the less, according to

[1] This enumeration, of which different versions are to be found in our earlier
works, is a synthesis deduced from the very nature of things. Sufism puts
forward various classifications of the virtues and distinguishes among them
exceedingly subtle ramifications; clearly it also insists on the apophatic nature
of the supernatural virtues and sees in these concomitances of the Spirit so
many 'stations' (*maqāmat*). Nature provides us with many pictures both of
the virtues and of the manifestations of the Spirit. The dove, the eagle, the
swan and the peacock reflect respectively purity, strength, contemplative
peace and spiritual generosity.

[2] According to St Thomas Aquinas 'truth is the ultimate goal of the whole
universe and the contemplation of truth is the essential activity of wisdom. . . .
By their very nature the virtues do not necessarily form part of contemplation
but they are an indispensable condition for it.'

circumstances, they fulfil a very precious function either as a 'framework' or as 'spiritual suggestion', not to mention the ritual importance of the highest order which they can assume and, further, symbolism has the particular quality of combining the external and the internal, the sensory and the spiritual, and thus, in principle or in fact, goes beyond the function of serving merely as a 'background'.

Sacred art is first of all the visible and audible[1] form of Revelation and then also its indispensable liturgical vesture. The form must be an adequate expression of its content; in no case should it contradict it, it cannot be abandoned to the arbitary decisions of individuals, to their ignorance and their passions. But we must differentiate between different degrees in sacred art, different levels of absoluteness or of relativity,[2] and in addition we must take account of the relative character of form as such. The spiritual integrity of the form is a 'categorical imperative' but this cannot prevent the formal order from being subject to certain vicissitudes; the fact that the masterpieces of sacred art are sublime expressions of the Spirit must not make us forget that, as seen from the standpoint of this same Spirit, these very works already appear, in their more ponderous exteriorizations, as concessions to 'the world' and recall the saying in the Gospels: 'All they that take the sword shall perish with the sword.' Indeed, when the Spirit has need of such a degree of exteriorization, it is already well on the way to being lost; exteriorization as such bears within itself the poison of exteriority, and so of exhaustion, fragility and decrepitude; the masterpiece is as it were laden with regrets and is already a swan-song; one sometimes has the impression that through the very overplus of its perfections the art is there to make up for the absence of wisdom or of sanctity. The Desert Fathers had no need of colonnades and stained glass windows; but, on the

[1] For instance, the chanting of the Quran, which can be in various styles, is an art; a choice can be made between one style and another, but nothing whatever can be added to them; one can chant the Quran in certain ways, in others one cannot. The modes of chanting express different rhythms of the spirit.

[2] First there is sacred art in the strictest sense, as it appears in the Tabernacle of Moses, where God Himself prescribed both the form and the materials; then there is the sacred art which has been developed in conformity with a particular ethnic genius; and finally there are decorative aspects of sacred art in which the ethnic genius is more freely expressed, though always in conformity with a spirit that transcends it. Genius is nothing unless determined by a spiritual perspective.

other hand, those who today despise sacred art in the name of 'pure spirit' are the very people who least understand it and have most need of it.[1] Be this as it may nothing noble can ever be lost; all the treasures of art and those of nature too are found again, in perfection and infinitely, in the divine Bliss; a man who is fully conscious of this truth cannot fail to be detached from sensory crystallization as such.

But there is also the primordial symbolism of virgin nature; this is an open book, a revelation of the Creator, a sanctuary and even, in certain respects, a way. In every period sages and hermits have gone to seek nature; it was with nature that they felt far from the world and close to Heaven; innocent and pious, but none the less profound and terrible, nature was ever their refuge. Had we to make a choice between the most magnificent of temples and inviolate nature, it is the latter we should choose; the destruction of all the works of human hands would be nothing compared to the destruction of nature.[2] Nature offers both vestiges of the earthly Paradise and foreshadowings of the heavenly Paradise.

All the same, from another point of view, we can ask ourselves which is more precious, the high peaks of sacred art, inasmuch as they are direct inspirations from God, or the beauties of nature inasmuch as they are divine creations and symbols;[3] the language of nature is doubtless more primordial and more universal, but it is less human and less immediately intelligible than art; for it to be able to deliver its message more spiritual knowledge is needed, since external things are what

[1] Art is always a criterion for the 'discerning of spirits': real paganism shows up in the behaviour of its art, as for example in the naturalism of Greco-Roman art and, no less strikingly, in the gigantism at once brutal and effeminate of Babylonian sculpture. We may also note the nightmarish art of precolumbian Mexico in its decadence.

[2] In the art of the Far East, which is much less 'humanistic' than the arts of the West and of Near-Eastern antiquity, man's work remains profoundly linked with nature to the point of forming with it a sort of organic unity; the art of China and Japan does not include 'pagan' elements as do the ancient arts of the Mediterranean countries; in its essential manifestations it is never sentimental nor hollow and crushing.

[3] Should we put first such works as the hieratic Virgin at Torcello near Venice, the prayer-niches of gleaming red stone in the mosque of Cordova, the images of divinities of India and the Far East, or the high mountains, the seas, forests and deserts? Formulated thus the question is objectively insoluble; for each side—that of art and that of nature—there are pluses and minuses.

we are, not in themselves but in respect of their efficacy;[1] the relationship is here the same, or almost the same as that between traditional mythologies and pure metaphysic. The best answer to this problem is that sacred art, of which some particular saint 'has no need' personally, none the less exteriorizes his sanctity, or precisely that something which can make artistic exteriorization superfluous for that saint himself[2]; through art this sanctity or wisdom has become miraculously tangible with all its human *materia* which virgin nature could not provide; in a sense the 'dilating' and 'refreshing' virtue of nature is that it is not human but angelic. To say that one prefers the 'works of God' to the 'works of man' would however be to simplify the problem unduly, given that in any art meriting the epithet 'sacred' it is God who is the author; man is merely the instrument and what is human merely the material.[3]

The symbolism of nature is conjoint with our human experience: if the starry vault turns it is because the heavenly worlds revolve round God; the appearance of turning is due, not only to our position on earth, but also and above all, to a transcendent prototype which is by no means illusory and seems even to have created our position in space in order to enable our spiritual perspective to be what it is; thus the earthly illusion reflects a real situation, and this relationship is of the highest importance, for it shows that it is the myths—always closely linked with the Ptolemean astronomy—which have the final say. As we have already pointed out on other occasions modern science, while it clearly provides exact observations though ignorant of the meaning and bearing of symbols, could not *de jure* contradict mythological conceptions in what they contain of spiritual value; it only changes the symbolical data, or in other words destroys the empirical bases of the mythologies without being able to explain the significance of the new data. From our point of view this science superimposes a symbolism exceedingly complicated in its language on another that is

[1] This is also, though in a lesser degree, true of art, lesser precisely because the language of art passes through a man.

[2] 'Can make', not 'must make', since art can have for some saints a function that eludes the ordinary man.

[3] The image of the Buddha combines in the most expressive way the categories treated of here: knowledge and concentration, virtue (this being absorbed in the two preceding elements) tradition and art (represented by the image itself) and finally nature (represented by the lotus).

metaphysically just as true but more human (rather as though some treatise were translated into a more difficult language); but it does not know that it has discovered a language and that implicitly it is putting forward a new Ptolemaic metaphysic.

The wisdom of nature is to be found over and over again affirmed in the Quran, which insists on the 'signs' of creation for 'those endowed with understanding', and this indicates the relationship between nature and gnosis; the vault of heaven is the temple of the eternal *sophia*. The same word 'signs' (*ayāt*) also designates the verses of the Book; like the phenomena of nature, which is at once virginal and maternal, they reveal God as they spring forth from the 'Mother of the Book' and are transmitted by the virgin spirit of the Prophet.[1] Islam, like ancient Judaism, is particularly close to nature from the fact of being grounded in the nomadic spirit; its beauty is that of the desert and of the oasis; sand is for it a symbol of purity—sand is used for the ritual ablutions when water is lacking—while the oasis is a prefiguration of Paradise. The symbolism of sand is analogous to that of snow: it is a great unifying peace, like the *Shahādah* which is peace and light and finally dissolves the knots and antinomies of existence, or, by reabsorption, reduces all ephemeral coagulations to pure and immutable Substance. Islam arose from nature; the Sufis return to it, and this is one of the meanings of the *hadīth*: 'Islam began in exile and it will end in exile.' Towns, with their tendency to petrifaction and their seeds of corruption, are opposed to nature, which is ever virginal; their sole justification and the sole guarantee of their stability is to be sanctuaries; this guarantee is quite relative, for the Quran says: 'And there is no town that We (Allah) will not destroy, or will not severely punish, before the day of resurrection' (XVII, 60). All this enables us to understand why Islam sought, within the framework of an inevitable sedentarism, to maintain the spirit of nomadism; Moslem cities always retain the imprint of a journeying through space and time; everywhere Islam preserves the sacred sterility and austerity of the desert, but also, within this climate of death, the gay and precious overflowing of springs and of oases; the fragile grace of the mosques echoes the grace of the palm groves while the whiteness and monotony of the towns reflects the

Isn't Causality reversed?

---

[1] In the preceding chapter this was mentioned in what was said of the blessing of the Prophet.

beauty of the desert and so also of sepulchres. Beneath the emptiness of existence and behind its mirages lies the eternal profusion of Divine Life.

But let us return to our starting point, which was metaphysical truth as foundation of the way. Since this truth relates to esotericism—at any rate in those traditions where there is a polarity of esotericism and exotericism—we must here answer the question of knowing whether or not there exists an 'esoteric orthodoxy' or whether this expression is not rather a contradiction in terms or an abuse of language. The whole difficulty, in situations where it arises, lies in too narrow a conception of the term 'orthodoxy' on the one hand and of metaphysical knowledge on the other: it is in fact necessary to differentiate between two orthodoxies, the one extrinsic and formal and the other intrinsic and beyond form; the first relates to dogma and thus to form, the latter to universal truth and thus to essence. Now in esotericism these two are linked together in the sense that dogma is the key to direct knowledge; once such knowledge is attained we are evidently beyond form, but none the less esotericism is necessarily connected to the form which was its point of departure and the symbolism of which always remains valid.[1] For example Islamic esotericism will never reject the fundamentals of Islam, even if it happens incidentally to contradict some particular exoteric position or interpretation; we can even say that Sufism is orthodox thrice over, first because it is from the Islamic form and not from anywhere else that it takes wing, secondly because its realizations and doctrines correspond to truth and not to error and thirdly because it always remains conjoined with Islam, considering itself to be the 'marrow' (lubb) of Islam and not of some other religion. Despite his verbal audacity Ibn Arabi did not become a Buddhist, nor did he reject the dogmas and laws of the sharī'ah, and this amounts to saying that he did not leave orthodoxy, either that of Islam or that of Truth itself.

If some formulation appears to contradict a particular exoteric point of view, what matters is to know whether it is true or

[1] Herein lies one of the meanings of the Quranic injunction: 'Enter houses by their doors' (II, 189). There is no tarīqah without the sharī'ah. The latter is the circle and the former the radius; the haqīqah is the centre.

false, not whether it is 'conformist' or 'free'; in pure intellectuality the concepts of 'liberty', 'independence' or 'originality' are devoid of meaning, as moreover are their contraries. If the purest esotericism includes the whole truth—and that is the very reason for its existence—the question of 'orthodoxy' in the religious sense clearly cannot arise; direct knowledge of the mysteries could not be 'Moslem' or 'Christian', just as the sight of a mountain is the sight of a mountain and not something else; to speak of 'non-orthodox' esotericism is no less absurd for it would amount to holding, first that this esotericism was not conjoined to any form—in which case it would have neither authority nor legitimacy nor even any usefulness—and secondly that it was not the initiatic or 'alchemical' outcome of a revealed way, and so did not include a formal and 'objective' guarantee of any kind. These considerations should make it clear why the prejudice which attempts to explain everything in terms of 'borrowings' or 'syncretism' is ill founded, for the doctrines of wisdom, being true, cannot fail to be concordant; and if the basis is identical it must be that the expressions are so too. That some particularly happy expression may be echoed by a foreign doctrine is equally in the nature of things—the contrary would be abnormal and inexplicable—but that is no reason for generalizations based on this exceptional case or for pressing them to absurdity; that would be like concluding that, because sometimes things influence one another, all analogies in nature arise from unilateral or reciprocal influences.[1]

The question of the origins of Sufism is resolved by the fundamental discernment (furqān) of the Islamic doctrine:

---

[1] A similar error would have it that everything begins from written texts: this too is a most improper generalization. 'The Germans had a writing of their own, but, as Caesar noted to Lutetius, its use was strictly forbidden: all learning had to be passed on by word of mouth and retained in memory alone. In Peru down to relatively recent times, only knotted cords were tolerated' (Ernst Fuhrmann: *Reich der Inka*, Hagen 1922). Let us add this opinion of Plato's: 'All serious men will beware of treating of serious matters in writing'; however, according to the Rabbis, 'it is better to profane the Torah than to forget it' and similarly '. . . in these days those few old wise men still living among them (the Sioux) say that at the approach of the end of a cycle, when men everywhere have become unfit to understand and still more to realize the truths revealed to them at the origin . . . it is then permissible and even desirable to bring this knowledge out into the light of day, for by its own nature truth protects itself against being profaned and in this way it is possible it may reach those qualified to penetrate it deeply. . . .' (J. E. Brown: Foreword to *The Sacred Pipe*, University of Oklahoma Press).

God and the world; now there is something provisional about
this discernment arising from the fact that the divine Unity,
followed through to its ultimate consequences, precisely excludes
the duality formulated by every discernment, and it is in a sense
here that we find the starting point of the original and essential
metaphysic of Islam. One thing which must be taken into
account is that direct knowledge is in itself a state of pure
'consciousness' and not a theory; there is thus nothing sur-
prising in the fact that the complex and subtle formulations of
gnosis were not manifested from the very beginning and at a
single stroke, or that on occasion Neo-Platonic or Platonic concepts should have been borrowed for the purposes of dialectic.
Sufism is 'sincerity of faith' and this 'sincerity'—which has
absolutely nothing in common with the modern 'cult of sincerity'—is, on the level of doctrine, nothing other than an
intellectual vision that does not halt half-way but on the
contrary draws from the idea of Unity its most rigorous consequences: the final term of this is not only the idea of the nothingness of the world but also that of the supreme identity and the
corresponding realization: 'the unity of Reality' (*wahdat el-
Wujūd*).[1]

If for the Israelite or for the Christian perfection or sanctity
means 'to love the Lord thy God with all thy heart, and with all
thy soul, and with all thy might' (Deut. VI, 5) or 'and with all
thy mind' (διάνοια) (Matt. XXII, 37)—in the case of the
Israelite through the Torah and obedience to the Law and in
that of the Christian through the vocational sacrifice of 'love'—
for a Moslem perfection means to 'believe' with his whole being
that 'there is no god save God', a total faith of which the scriptural expression is the *hadīth* already quoted: 'Spiritual virtue
(*ihsān*, the function of which is to render "sincere" both *imān* and
islām, faith and practice) consists in adoring God as if you saw
Him, and if you do not see Him, none the less He sees you'.[2]
Where Jew and Christian put intensity, and so totality, of love

---

[1] The realization, through 'transforming Virtue' (*ihsān*), of Unity (*Wāhi-
diyah, Ahadiyah*) is 'unification' (*tawhīd*).

[2] Since *ihsān* is synonymous with *tasawwuf* ('Sufism'), this *hadīth* is the very
definition of esotericism and clearly shows that in Islam esotericism is 'total
belief', given that the conviction that *la ilaha illā 'Llāh* is the pillar of the whole
religious edifice. Let us not forget that the Bible says of Abraham that God
counted his faith unto him for righteousness; now Islam readily refers back to
Abraham (*Seyyidunā Ibrāhīm*).

~~the Moslem puts 'sincerity',~~ and so totality, of faith, which in becoming realized becomes gnosis, union, the mystery of non-otherness.

Viewed from the angle of sapiential Islam Christianity can be considered as the doctrine of the sublime, not as that of the absolute; it is the doctrine of a sublime relativity[1] which saves by its very sublimity—here we have in mind the divine Sacrifice —but has its root none the less and necessarily in the Absolute and can consequently lead to the Absolute. If we set out from the idea that Christianity is 'the Absolute become relativity in order that the relative might become absolute'[2]—to paraphrase an ancient and well-known formula—we are fully in the realm of gnosis and the reservation 'felt' by Islam no longer applies. But what must also be said, more generally speaking and apart from gnosis, is that Christianity adopts a point of view in which consideration of the Absolute as such does not *a priori* arise; the emphasis is laid on the 'means' or the 'intermediary' which in a certain sense absorbs the end; or again, the end is as it were guaranteed by the divinity of the means. All this mounts to saying that Christianity is fundamentally a doctrine of Union, and it is evidently through this aspect that it joins up with the 'unitarianism' of Islam and especially of Sufism.[3]

In the history of Christianity there is a kind of latent nostalgia for what might be called the 'Islamic dimension' if we go back to the analogy between the three perspectives of 'fear', 'love' and 'gnosis'—the 'kingdoms' of the 'Father', the 'Son' and the 'Holy Ghost'—and the three forms of monotheism, the Judaic, the Christian and the Moslem. Islam is in fact, from the point of view of 'typology', the religious crystallization of gnosis, hence

[1] This is proved by the doctrine of the Trinitarian 'relationships'. But in this respect the Orthodox outlook seems less 'closed' than that of Catholicism, or a certain Catholicism.

[2] In the same way: if Christ is an 'objectivation' of the divine Intellect, the heart-intellect of the gnostic is a 'subjectivation' of Christ.

[3] The whole Christian perspective and the whole of Christic gnosis is summed up in this saying: '. . . as thou, Father, art in me, and I in thee that they also may be one in us. . . . And the glory which thou gavest me I have given them; that they may be one, even as we are one: I in them, and thou in me. . . .' (John, XVII, 21–23). Christ is like the saving Name of God in human form; all that can be said of the one is valid also of the other; or again, he is not only the Intellect which, as Light of the world, distinguishes between the Real and the unreal, but he is also, in the aspect of the 'external' and 'objective' divine manifestation, the divine Name (the 'Word') which by its 'redeeming' virtue brings about the reintegration of the non-real in the Real.

its metaphysical whiteness and its earthly realism. Protestant-
ism, with its insistence on 'The Book' and free will and its
rejection both of a sacramental priesthood and of the celibacy
of priests, is the most massive manifestation of this nostalgia,[1]
although in an anti-traditional and modern mode and in a purely
'typological' sense;[2] but there were other manifestations of it,
more ancient and more subtle, such as the movements of
Amalric of Bena or Joachim of Floris, both of the twelfth
century, not forgetting the Montanists of the second century.
In the same order of ideas it is well known that Moslems interpret the foretelling of the Paraclete in St John's Gospel as
referring to Islam, and, clearly without excluding the Christian
interpretation, this becomes understandable in the light of the
triad already alluded to of 'Fear—love—gnosis'. Were it to
be pointed out that there has certainly been within Islam an
inverse tendency towards the Christian possibility or 'the kingdom of the Son', we would reply that its traces must be sought
in the field of Shiah and of Bektashiyah, that is to say in a
Persian and Turkish climate.

In Vedantic terminology the fundamental enunciation of
Christianity is: '*Atmā* became *Māyā* in order that *Māyā* might
become *Atmā*'; that of Islam then is that 'there is no *Atmā* if it
be not the one *Atmā*' and, for the *Muhammadun Rasūlu 'Llah*:
'*Māyā* is the manifestation of *Atmā*'. In the Christian formulation there is something equivocal in the sense that *Atmā* and
Māyā are juxtaposed; it could be taken to mean that the latter
exists in its own full right alongside the former with an identical
reality and it is to this possible misunderstanding that Islam
replies in its own way. Or again: all theologies—or theosophies
—can, broadly speaking, be summed up in these two types:
God-Being and God-Consciousness, or God-Object and God-
Subject, or again: God as objective and 'absolutely other' and
God as subjective, both immanent and transcendent. Judaism
and Christianity belong to the first category; so does Islam,
taken as a religion, but at the same time it is as it were the

---

[1] It was at the same time a reaction of the German world against the Mediterranean and against Jewry. In any case, if Germanic theosophy—in so far as it
is valid—could blossom in a Protestant climate, it was thanks to the very
indirect analogies already mentioned and not by virtue of the anti-Catholicism
of the Lutherans.

[2] Analogously, the Jewish Messianic outlook is dangerously allied to the
modern ideology of progress, but this of course outside Judaic orthodoxy.

religious and 'objectivist' expression of God-Subject, and that
is why it imposes itself, not by phenomena or miracles, but by
its evidentness, the content or 'motor' of which is 'unity' and
thus absoluteness; and that is why there is a certain connection
between Islam and gnosis or 'the kingdom of the Spirit'. As for
the universal significance of '*Atmā* became *Māyā* in order that
Māyā might become *Atmā*', this is a question of the descent of
the Divine, of the Avatara, of the sacred Book, of the Symbol,
of the Sacrament, of Grace in every tangible form, and thus also
of the Doctrine or of the Name of God, and so we come back to
the *Muḥammadun Rasūlu 'Llāh*. The emphasis is laid, either on
the divine container as in Christianity—in which case the container has inevitably also an aspect of content,[1] and so of
'truth'—or on the content, 'truth', as in Islam, and still more
so in all forms of gnosis—and then the content inevitably
presents itself in the formal aspects of what contains, and so
of 'divine phenomenon' or of symbol.[2] The container is 'the
Word made flesh', and the content is the absoluteness of Reality
or the Self, expressed in Christianity by the injunction to love
God with the whole of our being and to love our neighbour as
ourself, 'all things being *Atmā*'.[3]

The diversity of religions and their equivalence in respect of
what is essential is due—according to the most intellectual Sufi
perspective—to the natural diversity of the collective receptacles: each individual receptacle having its own particular Lord,
the same will be true of psychological collectivities.[4] The 'Lord'

[1] 'I am the Way, the Truth and the Life. . . .'

[2] The Quran is an objective divine 'descent', a 'sign' and a 'mercy', and this
coincides with the meaning of the second *Shahādah*.

[3] Or Allah in His aspect of *Ezh-Zhāhir* ('The Outward') to use Sufi terminology.

[4] El-Hallaj says in his *Dīwān*: 'I have meditated on the various religions,
forcing myself to understand them, and I have found that they arise from a
unique principle having numerous ramifications. So do not ask of a man that
he should adopt this or that religion, for that would take him away from the
fundamental principle; it is this principle itself which must come to seek him;
in this principle are elucidated all heights and all meanings, then he (the man)
will understand them.' In translating this passage Massignon speaks of 'con-
fessional denominations' (for *adyan*), which is quite right in this context.
This universalism—prefigured in Judaism by Enoch, Melchisedec and Elias,
and in Christianity by the two saints John and also, at a lesser level, by the
'Christian' exorcist who did not follow Christ ('He that is not against us is for
us') and by the centurion of Capernaum—is personified in Islam by El-Khadir
or El-Khidr (Quran, XVIII, 60–82), the 'immortal' sometimes identified with
Elias, and by Uways El-Qaranī, a *ḥanīf* of the Yemen and patron of the
gnostics ('*ārifūn*).

is the Being-Creator inasmuch as He concerns or 'looks on' a particular soul or a particular category of souls and is regarded by them in function of their own natures, which in their turn are derived from particular divine possibilities, for God is 'The First' (*El-Awwal*) and 'The Last' (*El-Akhir*).

A religion is a form, and so also a limit, which 'contains' the Limitless, to speak in paradox; every form is fragmentary because of its necessary exclusion of other formal possibilities; the fact that these forms—when they are complete, that is to say when they are perfectly 'themselves'—each in their own way represent totality does not prevent them from being fragmentary in respect of their particularization and their reciprocal exclusion. In order to safeguard the axiom—metaphysically unacceptable—of the absolute character of this or that religious phenomenon people reach the point of denying both principial truth—to wit the true Absolute—and the intellect which becomes conscious of it, transferring to the phenomenon as such the characteristics of absoluteness and certitude proper to the Absolute and the Intellect alone, thus giving rise to philosophical endeavours which, though no doubt clever, thrive chiefly on their own inner contradiction. It is contradictory to base a certitude that demands to be considered as total, on the one hand on the phenomenal order and on the other on mystical grace while at the same time demanding an intellectual acceptance; a certitude belonging to the phenomenal order may be derived from a phenomenon, but a certitude of the principial order can only come from principles, whatever the occasional cause of the intellection, in a given case; if certitude can spring from intelligence—and it must be derived from it in the same degree as the truth to be known is profound —this is because through its fundamental nature it is already there.

From another angle we say that, if That which is in itself The Evident *in divinis* becomes Sacred Phenomenon in a particular order—in this case the human and historical order—that is above all because the predestined receptacle is a collectivity, and so a multiple subject differentiated in the individuals composing it and extending in time and beyond ephemeral individualities; the divergence of points of view is produced only from that moment when the sacred phenomenon becomes separated in the consciousness of men from the eternal truth it manifests—a truth no longer 'perceived'—and as a result certitude becomes 'belief' based exclusively on the phenomenon, on the objective divine sign, the external miracle, or—what amounts to the same thing—on the principle as grasped by the reason and reduced in practice to the phenomenon. When the sacred phenomenon as such becomes in practice the exclusive factor in certitude, the principial and supra-phenomenal intellect is brought down to the level of profane phenomena, as though pure intelligence were capable only of relativities and as though the 'supernatural' were some arbitrary act of Heaven and not in the very nature of things. When we differentiate between 'substance' and 'accidents' we conclude that phenomena relate to the latter and intellect to the former, but of course the religious phenomenon is a direct or central manifestation of the element 'substance', whereas the intellect, in its human actualization and from the point of view of expression alone, necessarily belongs to the accidentality of this world of forms and movements.

The fact that the intellect is a static and permanent grace makes it merely 'natural' in the eyes of some, which amounts to denying it; in the same order of ideas to deny the intellect because not everyone has access to it is just as false as to deny grace because not everyone enjoys it. Some would say that gnosis is Luciferian and tends to void religion of its content and to deny its quality of supernatural gift, but it could just as well be said that the attempt to lend a metaphysical absoluteness to religious concentration on phenomena, or to the exclusivism this implies, is a highly ingenious attempt to invert the normal order of things by denying—in the name of a certitude drawn from the phenomenal order and not from the principial and intellectual order—the evidence which the intellect bears within itself. The intellect is the criterion of phenomena; if the converse is also true it is however so in a more indirect sense and in a much more relative and external manner. At the beginning of a religion, or within a religious world that is still homogeneous, the problem does not in practice arise.

The proof of the cognitive transcendence of the intellect lies in the fact that, while dependent existentially on Being inasmuch as it is manifested, it can go beyond Being in a certain fashion since it is able to define Being as a limitation—for creation—of the Divine Essence, which Itself is 'Beyond-Being'.

145

or 'Self'. In the same way, to the question whether or not the intellect can 'place' itself above the religions, considered as spiritual and historical phenomena, or whether there exists outside the religions an 'objective' point allowing of an escape from a particular religious 'subjectivity', the answer is: yes, certainly, since the intellect can define religion and assess its formal limits; but it is obvious that if by the term 'religion' is meant the inner infinitude of Revelation, then the intellect cannot go beyond it, or rather the question then no longer arises, for the intellect participates in this infinitude and is even identified with it in respect of its intrinsic nature as where it is most strictly 'itself' and most difficult of access.

In the symbolism of the spider's web, to which we have already had occasion to refer in previous works, the radii represent essential 'identity' and the circles existential 'analogy', and this demonstrates in a very simple though adequate way the whole difference between the elements of 'intellection' and of 'phenomena' as well as their solidarity with one another and since, because of this solidarity, neither of the two elements shows itself in a pure state we could also speak—in order not to neglect any important shade of meaning—of 'continuous analogy' in the case of the former and of 'discontinuous identity' in the case of the latter. All certainty, and notably that concerning what is logically and mathematically evident—arises from the divine Intellect, the one and only intellect; but it arises from it through the existential or phenomenal screen of reason, or—to be more precise—through the screens which separate reason from its ultimate Source; it is the discontinuous identity of the sun's light which, even when filtered through a number of panes of coloured glass, always remains essentially the same light. As for the continuous analogy between phenomena and the Principle which breathes them forth, if it is clear that the phenomenon-symbol is not that which it symbolizes— the sun is not God and that is why it sets—its existence is none the less an aspect or mode of Existence as such;[1] this it is which allows us to call the analogy 'continuous' when we envisage it in relation to its ontological attachment to pure Being, although such terminology, here used in a quite provisional way, is logically contradictory and useless in practice. Analogy is a

---

[1] But not, of course, a 'part' of Existence.

discontinuous identity and identity a continuous analogy;[1] once again, here is the whole difference between the sacred or symbolic phenomenon and principial intellection.[2]

Gnosis has been reproached with being an exalting of the 'human intelligence'; in this last expression the error can be caught on the wing, for metaphysically intelligence is, above all, intelligence and nothing else; it is only human to the degree that it is no longer altogether itself, that is, when from being substance it has become accident. For man, and indeed for every being, there are two relationships to be envisaged: that of the 'concentric circle' and that of the 'centripetal radius';[3] according to the first, intelligence is limited appropriately to a determinate existence and then envisaged in so far as it is separated from its source or is only a refraction of that source, according to the second intelligence is all that it is by its intrinsic nature whatever its contingent situation in any particular case. The intelligence discernible in plants—to the extent that it is infallible—'is' the intelligence of God, the only intelligence there is; this is even more clearly true of the intelligence of man, where it is capable of loftier equivalences thanks to its being at once integral and transcendent. There is but one subject, the universal Self, and its existential refractions or ramifications are either itself or not itself according to the relationship envisaged. This truth one may either understand or not understand; it cannot be accommodated to everyone's requirements of causal relationship just as it is impossible to bring within reach of everyone such ideas as that of the 'relatively absolute' or of the metaphysical transparency of phenomena. Pantheists would say that 'all is God' with the unspoken thought that God is nothing more than the sum of all things; true metaphysic on the contrary says both that 'all is God' and that 'nothing is God', adding that God is nothing except Himself and that He is

[1] Identity presupposes two terms, and those precisely which show themselves identical—unilaterally and irreversibly: that is to say that at the basis of an apparent diversity there is a single reality, whence the character of analogy.

[2] One could specify by speaking of 'continuity accidentally discontinuous' and of 'discontinuity essentially continuous', the former referring to intellect and the latter to phenomena, to the symbol, to objective manifestation.

[3] Herein lies the whole difference between analogy and essential identity, the one being always an aspect of the other.

nothing of that which is in the world. There are truths only expressible through antinomies but this does not at all mean that in this case they constitute a philosophical procedure which ought to lead to some 'conclusion' or other, for direct knowledge stands above the contingencies of reason; vision must not be confused with expression. After all truths are profound, not because they are difficult to express for one who knows them, but because they are difficult to understand for one who does not know them; hence the disproportion between the simplicity of the symbol and the possible complexity of the mental operations.

To suggest, as do some, that in gnosis intelligence sets itself presumptuously in the place of God is to ignore the fact that it could not within the field of its own nature realize what we might call the 'being' of the Infinite; pure intelligence does communicate an adequate and efficacious reflection—or system of reflections—of it, but does not directly transmit the divine 'being' itself; were it otherwise intellectual knowledge would immediately identify us with its object. The difference between belief and gnosis, between elementary religious faith and metaphysical certainty, is comparable to the difference between a description of a mountain and direct vision of it: the second no more puts us on the mountain top than does the first, but it does inform us about the properties of the mountain and the route to follow; let us not however forget that a blind man who walks without stopping advances more quickly than a normal man who stops at each step. Be this as it may, sight identifies the eye with light, communicating a correct and homogeneous knowledge[1] and making possible the taking of short-cuts where the blind would have to feel his way; and this should be said even if it displeases those moralistic decriers of the intellect who refuse to admit that it too is a grace, though static and 'naturally supernatural' in its mode.[2] However, as

[1] To the objection that even those in whom we recognize the quality of traditional metaphysicians can contradict one another we would reply that this may be so in the field of applications where a man may always be ignorant of facts, but never on the plane of pure principles which alone have an absolutely decisive bearing, whatever their level.

[2] The human condition, with all that distinguishes it from animality, is likewise such a grace. If there is here a certain abuse of language, it is metaphysical truth which forces us to it, the reality of things not being subject to the limitations of words.

has already been pointed out, intellection is assuredly not the whole of gnosis, since this includes the mysteries of union and, it might be said, opens out directly on the the Infinite; the 'uncreated' character of the Sufi in the full sense (*eṣ-Sūfī lam yukhlaq*) *a priori* concerns only the transpersonal essence of the intellect and not that state of absorption in the Reality which the intellect makes us 'perceive' or of which it makes us 'aware'. Total gnosis goes immensely beyond all that appears in man as 'intelligence' precisely because it is an incommensurable mystery of 'being'; here we have the whole difference, indescribable in human language, between vision and realization; in the latter 'seeing' becomes 'being' and our existence is transmuted into light. But even ordinary intellectual vision—the intellection which reflects, assimilates and discerns without necessarily bringing about ontological transmutation—is already something which goes far beyond mere thought, the discursive and 'philosophical' play of the mind.

Metaphysical or esoteric dialectic moves between the simplicity of symbolism and reflective complexity; now this latter —though modern man has difficulty in understanding the point —can become more and more subtle without for all that getting one inch nearer to truth; in other words a thought may be subdivided into a thousand ramifications and fenced round with all possible precautions and yet remain external and 'profane', for no virtuosity of the potter will transform clay into gold. It is possible to conceive of a language a hundred times more elaborated than that which is used today, for here no principial limitation intervenes; every formulation is necessarily 'naïve' in its way and it is always possible to try to enhance it by luxuriance of logical or imaginative word-play; and this proves on the one hand that elaboration as such adds no essential quality to an enunciation, and on the other hand, retrospectively, that the relatively simple enunciations of sages of former times were charged with a fullness of meaning which is precisely what people today no longer know how to discern and the existence of which they are indeed very ready to deny. It is not an elaboration of thought pressed to the point of absurdity which can lead us to the heart of reality; those who think to proceed on this plane by investigations and gropings, scrutinizing things and weighing them up, have failed to grasp that we cannot subject all orders of knowledge to the same 'regimen' of logic and experiment and that there are realities which are either understood at a glance or else not understood at all.

Not unconnected with what has just been said is the question of the two wisdoms, the one metaphysical and the other mystical; it would be entirely wrong to take certain mystical or 'unitive' formulations as authority for denying the legitimacy of intellectual definitions, wrong at any rate for anyone who is himself outside the special state in question, for in fact it does come about that certain contemplatives, speaking in the name of direct experience, reject doctrinal formulations, these having become for them 'words', which does not always prevent them from putting forward other formulations of the same order and having in the event the same value.[1] Here we must avoid confusing the strictly intellectual or doctrinal plane, which has all the legitimacy and so all the efficacy conferred on it by the nature of things, with the plane of inner experience, the plane of ontological 'perceptions' or of the 'perfumes' or 'savours' of the mysteries; it would be quite as wrong as to dispute the adequacy of a map because one had undertaken an actual journey or, for example, to pretend, because one had travelled from North to South, that the Mediterranean was at the top and not at the bottom as shown on the map.

Metaphysics has as it were two grand dimensions, the one ascending and dealing with universal principles and the distinction between the Real and the illusory, and the other descending and dealing on the contrary with the 'divine life' in creaturely situations, and thus with the fundamental and secret 'divinity' of beings and of things, for 'all is *Atmā*'; the first dimension can be called 'static' and is related to the first *Shahādah* and to 'extinction' (*fanā*), to 'annihilation' (*istihlāk*), whereas the second has a 'dynamic' air and is related to the second *Shahādah* and to 'permanence' (*baqā*). By comparison with the first dimension the second is mysterious and paradoxical, seeming at certain points to contradict the first, and again, it is like a wine with which the Universe becomes intoxicated; but it must never be lost sight of that this second dimension is already implicitly contained within the first— even as the second *Shahādah* is derived from the first, to wit

[1] In *The Transcendent Unity of Religions* a characteristic of this kind was noted in the *Risālat el-Ahadiyah* ('Treatise on The Unity') attributed, rightly or wrongly, to Ibn Arabī but in any case depending directly on his doctrine.

from the 'point of intersection' *illā*—so that static, 'elementary' or 'separative' metaphysics is sufficient unto itself and does not merit any reproach from those who savour the intoxicating paradoxes of the unitive experience. That which in the first *Shahādah* is the word *illā* will be in the first metaphysics the concept of universal causality: we start out from the idea that the world is false since the Principle alone is real, but since we are in the world we add the reservation that the world reflects God; and it is from this reservation that the second metaphysics springs forth and according to its point of view the first is like an insufficient dogmatism. Here in a sense we see the confrontation of the perfections of incorruptibility and of life: the one cannot be had without the other, and it would be a pernicious 'optical error' to despise doctrine in the name of realization, or to deny the latter in the name of the former. However, since the first error is more dangerous than the second—the second moreover hardly arises in pure metaphysics and, if it does, consists in overestimating the 'letter' of the doctrine in its formal particularism—we would recall this saying of Christ; for the glory of doctrine: 'Heaven and earth shall pass away, but my words shall not pass away.' The Hindu, or Hindu and Buddhist, theory of the *upayas* perfectly takes account of these dimensions of the spiritual realm: concepts are true according to the levels to which they relate; it is possible to go beyond them, but they never cease to be true at their own level, and that level is an aspect of Absolute Reality.

In the sight of the Absolute, envisaged as pure Self and unthinkable Aseity, metaphysical doctrine is assuredly tinged with relativity, but it none the less offers absolutely sure reference points and 'adequate approximations' such as the human spirit could not do without; and this is what the simplifiers who pursue the 'concrete' are incapable of understanding. Doctrine is to the Truth what the circle or the spiral is to the centre.

The idea of the 'subconscious' is susceptible, not only of a psychological and lower interpretation, but also of a spiritual, higher, and consequently purely qualitative interpretation. It is true that in this case one should speak of the 'supra-conscious' but the fact is that the supra-conscious has also an aspect that is 'subterranean' in relation to our ordinary consciousness, just as the heart resembles a submerged sanctuary which, symbolically speaking, reappears on the surface thanks to unitive realization; it is this subterranean aspect that allows us to speak—in a provisional way—of a 'spiritual subconscious' which must never for one moment be taken to mean the lower, vital psyche, the passive and chaotic dreaming of individuals and collectivities.

This spiritual subconscious, as here understood, is formed of all that the intellect contains in a latent and implicit fashion; now the intellect 'knows' through its very substance all that is capable of being known and, like the blood flowing through even the tiniest arteries of the body, it traverses all the egos of which the universe is woven and opens out 'vertically' on the Infinite. In other words: the intellective centre of man, which is in practice 'subconscious', has knowledge, not only of God, but also of man's nature and his destiny;[1] and this enables us to present Revelation as a 'supernaturally natural' manifestation of that which the human species 'knows', in its virtual and submerged omniscience, both about itself and about God. Thus the Prophetic phenomenon appears as a kind of awakening, on the human plane, of the universal consciousness that is present everywhere in the cosmos in varying degrees of opening up or of slumber. But as humanity is diverse, this upspringing of knowledge is also diverse, not in respect of its essential content but in respect of its form, and this is an aspect of the 'instinct of self-preservation' of collectivities or of their 'subconscious' wisdom; for the saving truth must correspond to its receptacles, it must be intelligible and efficacious for each one of them. In Revelation it is always in the last analysis the 'Self' which speaks and, as its Word is eternal, the human receptacles 'translate' it—at their root and by their nature, not consciously or deliberately—into the language of particular spatial and temporal conditions[2]; individualized consciousnesses

[1] The predictions, not only of the prophets but also of shamans in a state of trance, are explained by this cosmic homogeneity of the intelligence, and so of 'knowing'; the shaman knows how to put himself in contact with a subconscious which contains facts past and future, and sometimes penetrates into the regions of the world beyond.

[2] This means that the 'translation' is already wrought in God with a view to a given human receptacle; it is not the receptacle which determines God, but God who predisposes the receptacle. In the case of indirect inspiration (San-

are so many veils which filter and adapt the blinding light of unconditioned Consciousness, of the Self.[1] For Sufic gnosis the whole of creation is a play, with infinitely varied and subtle combinations, of cosmic receptacles and divine unveilings.

This object of these considerations is, not to add one speculation to other speculations, but to give the reader some inkling—even if every mentality is not satisfied—that the phenomenon of religion, wholly supernatural though it is by definition, has also a 'natural' side to it which in its own way guarantees the truthfulness of the phenomenon; by this we mean that religion—or wisdom—is connatural with man and that man would not be man were there not included in his nature a field of flowering for the Absolute, or again that he would not be man—'the image of God'—if his nature did not allow him to become conscious, despite his 'petrifaction' and through it, of all that 'is' and so also of all that is in his ultimate interest. Thus Revelation manifests all the intelligence that virginal things possess and is by analogy assimilable—though on an immeasurably higher level—to the infallibility which directs birds on their migration to the South and draws plants towards the light;[2] it is all that we know in the virtual plenitude of our being, and it is also all that we love and all that we are.

Before the loss of the harmony of Eden primordial man saw things from within, in their substantiality and in the divine Unity; after the Fall he no longer saw them except externally and in their accidentality, and so outside God. Adam is the spirit (*rūh*) or the intellect (*'aql*) and Eve the soul (*nafs*); it is

skrit: *smriti*)—the case of the sacred commentaries—which must not be confused with 'Revelation' (*shruti*), the part played by the receptacle is not simply existential, but active in the sense that it 'interprets' according to the Spirit instead of 'receiving' directly from the Spirit.

[1] They do so in two ways or at two degrees according to whether it is a case of direct or indirect, divine or sapiential, inspiration.

[2] The allusion here is not simply to the intuition which leads believers to follow the heavenly Message, but to the 'natural supernature' of the human species which attracts Revelations in the same way as in nature a given container attracts a corresponding content. As for the 'naturally supernatural'—or the converse, which in the whole comes to the same thing—it may be added that the Angels form a complementary example in relation to the Intellect: the Angels are the 'objective' channels for the Holy Spirit just as the Intellect is its 'subjective' channel; these two kinds of channel are moreover merged in the sense that every intellection passes through *Er-Rūh*, the Spirit.

through the soul—'horizontal' complement of the 'vertical' spirit and existential pole of pure intelligence—or through the will that the movement towards exteriorization and dispersion came; the tempter serpent, which is the cosmic genius of this movement, cannot act directly on the intelligence and so must seduce the will, Eve. When the wind blows over a perfectly still lake the sun's reflection is disturbed and broken up, and it is thus that the loss of Eden was brought about, thus that the divine reflection was broken up. The Way means return to the vision enjoyed by innocence, to the inward dimension where all things die and are reborn in the divine Unity—in that Absolute which, with its concomitances of equilibrium and inviolability, is the whole content of the human condition and the whole reason for its existence.

And this innocence is also the 'childhood' which 'takes no heed for the morrow'. The Sufi is the 'son of the moment' (*ibn el-waqt*), which means, first of all, that he is conscious of eternity and that through his 'remembrance of God' he remains in the 'timeless instant' of 'heavenly actuality'; but it means also and consequentially, that he keeps himself all the time in the divine Will, that is to say, he realizes that the present moment is what God wants of him; therefore he will not desire to be 'before' or 'after' or to enjoy that which is in fact outside the divine 'now'—that irreplaceable instant in which we belong concretely to God and which is indeed the only instant when we can in fact want to belong to Him.

At this point we wish to give a concise summary, but one as exact as possible, of what fundamentally constitutes 'the Way' in Islam. At the same time this conclusion of the book will once more underline the strictly Quranic and Muhammedan character of the Sufic Way.[1]

First let us recall this crucial fact: *tasawwuf* coincides according to tradition with *ihsān* and *ihsān* is 'that thou shouldest adore God as if thou didst see Him and, if thou dost not see Him, yet He seeth thee'. *Ihsān—tasawwuf*—is nothing other than the perfectly 'sincere' (*mukhlisah*) 'adoration'

[1] The dialectical borrowings, which were always possible and even inevitable as a result of contact with the wisdom of Greece, add nothing to the intrinsic *haqīqah* of *tasawwuf*, but only throw light on it.

(*'ibādah*) of God, the bringing intelligence-will into full accord with its 'content' and divine prototype.[1]

The quintessence of adoration—and so, in a certain sense, adoration as such—is to believe that *lā ilahā illā 'Llāh* and, as a consequence, that *Muhammadun rasūlu 'Llāh*. The proof of this is that according to Islamic dogma and within its 'radius of jurisdiction', a man is only certainly damned by reason of the absence of this faith. The Moslem is not *ipso facto* damned because he does not pray or does not fast; he may indeed be prevented from doing so and in certain physical conditions women are exempted from these requirements; nor is he necessarily damned because he does not pay the tithe: the poor —and especially beggars—are exempted from it, which is at least an indication of a certain relativity both in this and in the preceding cases. Still more clearly a man is not damned through the mere fact of not having accomplished the Pilgrimage; the *muslim* is only bound to make the Pilgrimage if he is able to do so; as for the holy war, it is not always being waged and, even when it is, the sick, invalids, women and children are not bound to participate in it. But a man is necessarily damned—still within the framework of Islam or else in a transposed sense— for not believing that *lā ilaha illā 'Llāh* and that *Muhammadun rasūlu 'Llāh*;[2] this law knows no exception, for it is identified in a way with that which makes the very meaning of the human condition. Thus it is indisputably this faith which constitutes the quintessence of Islam; and it is the 'sincerity' (*ikhlāṣ*) of this faith or this acceptance which constitutes *ihsān* or *taṣawwuf*. In other words; it is strictly conceivable that a *muslim* who had, for example, all his life omitted to pray or to fast, might despite everything be saved and that for reasons that elude us but which would count in the eyes of the Divine Mercy; on the other hand it is inconceivable that a man who denied that *lā ilaha illā 'Llāh* should be saved since this negation would quite clearly deprive him of the very quality of *muslim*, and so of the *conditio sine qua non* of salvation.

Now the sincerity of faith also implies its depth, according

---

[1] The Shaikh El-Allaoui, following the current terminology of the Sufis, specifies that the beginning of *ihsān* is 'vigilance' (*murāqabah*) whereas its end is 'direct contemplation' (*mushāhadah*).

[2] In the climate of Christianity it would be said that this was the 'sin against the Holy Ghost'.

to a man's capacity; and to speak of capacity is to speak of vocation.[1] We must understand to the same degree that we are intelligent, not to a degree that we are not so and where there is no possibility of bridging the gap between the knowing subject and the level of the object to be known. The Bible also teaches, in both the Old and the New Testaments, that we must 'love' God with all our faculties; so intelligence could not be excluded from this, the more so since it is intelligence which characterizes man and distinguishes him from the animals. Free will would be inconceivable apart from intelligence.

Man is made of integral or transcendent intelligence—and therefore capable of abstraction just as well as of suprasensory intuition—and of free will and that is why there is a truth and a way, a doctrine and a method, a faith and a submission, an *imān* and an *islām*; *ihsān*, being the perfection and the final term of these two, is at the same time in them and above them. It can also be said that there is an *ihsān* because there is in man something which calls for totality, or something absolute or infinite.

The quintessence of the truth is discernment between the contingent and the Absolute; and the quintessence of the way is permanent consciousness of Absolute Reality. Now to say 'quintessence' is to say '*ihsān*', in the spiritual context here in question.

Man, as has just been said, is made of intelligence and will; so he is made of understandings and virtues, of things he knows and things he does, or in other words of what he knows and what he is. The understandings are prefigured in the first *Shahādah* and the virtues in the second; that is why *tasawwuf* can be described either by expounding a metaphysic or by commenting on the virtues. The second *Shahādah* is in essence identifiable with the first, of which it is only a prolongation, just as the virtues are fundamentally identifiable with truths and are in a sense derived from them. The first *Shahādah*—that of God—enunciates every principial truth; the second *Shahādah* —that of the Prophet—enunciates every fundamental virtue.

The essential truths are as follows: that of the Essence

[1] However, God does not require from us on this level that we should reach the goal we conceive of and pursue because we conceive of it and because of its truth; as the Bhagavadgītā clearly teaches, God here requires only effort and does not punish for lack of success.

divine and 'one' (*Dhāt, Ayadiyah* in the sense of the 'non-duality' of the Vedanta); then the truth of Being which creates (*Khāliq*), a Principle that is also 'one'—but in the sense of an 'affirmation' and by virtue of an 'auto-determination' (*Wahidiyah*, 'solitude', 'oneness')—and comprising, if not 'parts',[1] at least aspects or qualities.[2] On the hither side of the principial or divine realm there is on the one hand the macrocosm with its 'archangelic' and 'quasi-divine' centre *Rūh*, 'Spirit', and on the other hand, at the extreme periphery of its deployment that coagulation—of universal Substance—which we call 'matter' and which is for us the outer shell, at once innocent and deadly, of existence.

As for the essential virtues, which we have treated of elsewhere though they must also figure in this final summing up, they are the perfections of 'fear', 'love' and 'knowledge', or in other words those of 'poverty', 'generosity' and 'sincerity'; in a sense they make up *islām* as the truths make up *imān*, their deepening—or their qualitative final term—constituting the nature or the fruit itself of *ihsān*. Again, it could be said that the virtues consist fundamentally in fixing oneself in God according to a king of symmetry or triadic rhythm, fixing oneself in Him 'now', 'here' and 'thus'; but these images can also replace one another, each being sufficient in itself.

The Sufi remains in the timeless 'present' where there are no longer regrets or fears; he remains at the limitless 'centre' where the outer and the inner are blended or outpassed; or again, his 'secret' is the perfect 'simplicity' of every virginal Substance. Being only 'what he is' he is all 'That which is'.

The simplicity of a substance is its indivisibility. The symbolism here evoked perhaps requires clarifying as follows: if the conditions of bodily existence are time, space, substance that is material or has become such, form and number, the three last-named—matter, form and number—are the content of the first two—time and space. Form and number coincide

---

[1] For that would be contrary to the indivisiblity and non-associability of the Principle.

[2] God is not 'in existence'—He is beyond Existence—but He can be said to be 'not inexistent' if one is concerned to underline the evident fact that He is 'real' without being 'existent'. In no case can it be said of God that He is 'inexistent'; He is 'non-existent' inasmuch as He does not depend on the existential domain, but 'non-inexistent' inasmuch as His transcendence evidently could not involve any privation.

in a sense, and on the plane in question, with matter, of which they are respectively the outer determinations of quality and quantity; the inner corresponding determinations are on the one hand the nature of the *materia* envisaged and on the other hand its extent. Like the idea of 'substance' the four other concepts of an existential condition can be applied beyond the sensory field; they are not terrestrial accidents but reflections of universal structures.

If man is will, God is Love; if man is intelligence, God is Truth. If man is will fallen and powerless, God is redeeming Love; if man is intelligence darkened and gone astray, God is the illuminating Truth which delivers; for it is in the nature of knowledge—the bringing of intelligence to the level of truth—to render pure and free. The divine Love saves by 'making Itself' what we are, it 'descends' in order to 'raise up'; the divine Truth delivers by giving back to the intellect Its 'supernaturally natural' object and so also its first purity, that is to say by 'recalling' that the Absolute alone 'is', that contingency 'is not' or that on the contrary 'it is not other than the Absolute' in respect of pure Existence and also, in certain cases, in respect of pure Intelligence or 'Consciousness' and in respect of strict Analogy.

Analogy or Symbolism concerns all manifestation of qualities; Consciousness concerns man inasmuch as he can intellectually go beyond himself, his spirit opening out in the Absolute; as for Existence it concerns all things—whether qualitative or not and whether conscious or not—by the simple fact that they are separated from nothingness, it might be said. Phenomena are 'neither God nor other than He': they possess nothing of themselves, neither existence nor positive attributes; they are divine qualities 'eroded' in an illusory manner by nothingness—itself non-existent—by reason of the infinitude of universal Possibility.

The *Shahādah*, by which Allah manifests Himself as Truth, addresses itself first of all to the intelligence, but also, and as a consequence, to that extension of intelligence which is the will. When the intelligence grasps the fundamental meaning of the *Shahādah* it distinguishes the Real from the non-real, or 'Substance' from 'accidents'; when the will in its turn grasps this same meaning it becomes attached to the Real, to the divine 'Substance'; it becomes concentrated and lends its concentration to the mind. Intelligence enlightened by the *Shahādah* has in the last analysis but one single object or content, Allah, other objects or contents being considered only in function of Him or in relation to Him, so that the multiple becomes as it were plunged in the One; and the same is true of the will, according to what God may bestow on the creature. The 'remembrance' of God is logically a function of the rightness of our idea of God and of the depth of our comprehension: Truth, to the degree that it is essential and that we understand it, takes possession of our whole being and little by little transforms it according to a discontinuous and unforeseeable rhythm. Becoming crystallized in us It 'makes Itself what we are in order to make us what It is'. The manifestation of Truth is a mystery of Love, just as, conversely, the content of Love is a mystery of Truth.

In all these considerations it has been our aim not to give a picture of Moslem esotericism in its historical deployment, but to bring it to its most elemental positions by connecting it with the very roots of Islam which of necessity are its own. It was not so much a matter of recapitulating what Sufism may have said as of saying what it is and has never ceased to be through all the complexity of its developments. This way of looking at things has enabled us—perhaps to the detriment of the apparent coherence of this book—to dwell at some length on meeting points with other traditional perspectives and also on the structure of what is—around us as well as within us—both divinely human and humanly divine.